Leading Insights

Special Education and Inclusion

© 2021 by the Association of Christian Schools International

All rights reserved. No portion of this book may be reproduced, stored in a retrieval system, or transmitted, in any form or by any means—mechanical, photocopying, recording, or otherwise—without prior written permission of ACSI.

Views expressed in this book are those of the contributing authors, and do not necessarily represent the views of the editors or the position of the Association of Christian Schools International.

Unless otherwise indicated, Scripture quotations are from the ESV® Bible (The Holy Bible, English Standard Version®), copyright © 2001 by Crossway Bibles, a publishing ministry of Good News Publishers. Used by permission. All rights reserved.

Other Scripture references are from *The Holy Bible*, New International Version @1973, 1984 by International Bible Society. Used by permission. All rights reserved.

Printed in the United States of America
27 26 25 24 23 22 21   1 2 3 4 5 6 7
Edited by Swaner, Lynn E.

ACSI Leading Insights: Special Education and Inclusion
ISBN 978-1-58331-516-3
eISBN 978-1-58331-562-0
Catalog#: 6680
     e6680
Designer: Lisa Ruppert
Copyeditor: Lora Schrock

Association of Christian Schools International
731 Chapel Hills Drive • Colorado Springs, CO 80920
Care Team: 800.367.0798 • www.acsi.org

CONTENTS

Introduction
    Lynn E. Swaner 4

Part I: Philosophy and Research

    1. A Biblical Case for Inclusion
        Thomas L. Boehm 8

    2. Creating Communities of Belonging
        Erik W. Carter, Elizabeth Lucas Dombrowski,
        Thomas L. Boehm 21

    3. A Review of the Research on Inclusive
       Christian Education
        Kate E. Strater 38

Part II: Perspectives on Inclusive Education

    4. The Student Perspective
        Elizabeth Lucas Dombrowski 51

    5. The Parent Perspective
        Matthew H. Lee 57

    6. The Head of School Perspective
        Interview with Rick Kempton 61

Part III: Shaping Our Practice

    7. The Inclusion Journey: From Program to Identity
        Elizabeth Lucas Dombrowski, Kate E. Strater 70

    8. Reimagining Finance and Sustainability:
       From Limits to Possibilities
        Elizabeth Lucas Dombrowski, Matthew H. Lee 85

Recommended Resources 96

References 116

About the Authors 127

Introduction

Lynn E. Swaner, *Series Editor*

Because of their biblically based philosophy of education, Christian schools ground their vision and mission in Scripture. This foundation should extend to how Christian schools engage students with disabilities, who are created in God's image (Gen. 1:27), have unique gifts bestowed by God (Eph. 2:10), and are invaluable members of Christ's body (1 Cor. 12:12-27). And yet, Christian schools across the United States often struggle to even make room for students with disabilities on their campuses: a 2019 nationwide survey of nearly 750 schools, conducted by the Association of Christian Schools International (ACSI), found that only 35 percent offered special education programs or related services (ACSI 2019).

The goal of this inaugural issue of ACSI *Leading Insights*, focused on special education and inclusion in Christian education,[1] is to encourage and equip all Christian schools to grow in their capacity to welcome students with disabilities—and in doing so, move our schools closer to becoming the kind of faith-filled communities where students of all abilities belong and flourish. The path to inclusion is not an easy one, but the experts who serve as chapter authors for this monograph share abundant insight from theology, research, and practice in Christian schools to guide leaders and teachers along the way. Between them, Thomas Boehm of Wheaton College, Erik Carter of Vanderbilt University, Kate Strater of Calvin College, and Elizabeth Lucas Dombrowksi of All Belong (a center for inclusive Christian education) identify a number of "from—to" journeys on which schools must embark:

---

[1] Historically, the term "inclusion" has denoted educational experiences that enable full participation of students with disabilities in schools. While the term has more recently been applied to other populations, the authors in this monograph use the term in its historical sense, as exclusively referencing students with disabilities.

from a view of inclusion as a lofty but impractical ideal, to understanding it as a *biblical mandate that is achievable in Christian schools;*

- from the exclusion and isolation experienced by many students with disabilities and their families, to genuine *embrace and belonging that reflects the heart of God*;

- from special education as a unidirectional effort to meet the needs of students with disabilities, to inclusion as a reflection of the reality that *students of any and all abilities bless each other and us* when they are present in our schools;

- from a programs-focused approach as a piecemeal way of serving only a small subset of students, to a s*choolwide identity as a site of inclusive education* for all families who desire it; and

- from financial and staffing limitations that hinder many schools, to the *limitless possibilities that arise from sustainable practices and faith-filled planning.*

In addition, this monograph shares crucial voices that need to be heard in the discussion of inclusion in Christian schools—from two alumni of inclusive Christian schools, Alex and Abby, who discuss the impact of inclusion on their lives and faith; Matt Lee, ACSI's Director of Research, who as a parent of a child with a disability shares hopes and dreams for one day enrolling her in a Christian school; and a long-serving head of school and ACSI Board member, Rick Kempton, who has successfully led two Christian schools along the inclusion journey. Their voices not only serve to bring the discussion around inclusion in Christian schools to life, but also help to broaden our collective imagination for what is possible in our schools.

We conclude this monograph with a selection of helpful resources and references that are intended to inspire and support the journey toward inclusion in Christian schools. When it comes to fulfilling our schools' biblically based missions for students with disabilities—and creating gospel-centered communities of faith for all students and families—may we believe and act in accordance with the biblical promise, that our "God will supply every need of yours according to his riches in glory in Christ Jesus" (Phil. 4:19).

Part I:
Philosophy and Research

A Biblical Case for Inclusive Christian Schools
Thomas L. Boehm, *Wheaton College*

Introduction

Since 1975, public schools in the United States have been mandated to serve students with disabilities through what is now known as the Individuals with Disabilities Education Improvement Act (IDEA). Christian schools, however, are not under the same legal mandate. How then should Christian schools respond to the needs of students with disabilities especially given private schools' limited financial and personnel resources? While Christian schools may not be under a legal mandate to serve students with disabilities, arguably they are under a higher mandate.

This chapter attempts to explore this mandate within a biblical context by presenting a concise theology of disability, composed of nine "pillars" of scriptural wisdom from Genesis to Revelation that offer a solid rationale and foundation upon which to build capacity to enroll and support students with disabilities. Each pillar is first framed by a brief biblical summary,[1] followed by a concise application statement for inclusive Christian schools that is further developed in the remainder of the section.

---

[1] These nine pillars are taken from the newly created Wheaton Center for Faith and Disability where we've summarized this biblical theology in collaboration with a diverse range of scholars and practitioners (see https://www.wheaton.edu/wheaton-center-for-faith-and-disability/about/biblical-theology-of-disability/). I would specifically like to thank Sandy Hay, Stephanie Hubach, Mark Talbot, Stan Jones, Michael Graves, Aubrey Buster, and David Hudson for their valuable insights and feedback on this initial version of a biblical theology of disability. Where faithful to Scripture, their contributions were instrumental; where errors remain they are the sole responsibility of the author.

Pillar 1: God's Image Bearers—A Glorious Reflection

Genesis 1:26–27 tells us that all people are made in the image of God, as the pinnacle act of His creation. We image God as integrated persons of body and soul/spirit. We each bear God's image individually. We also, however, image God collectively. As image bearers, our glorious task is to reflect God's character into the world—through all our words and deeds—not only individually, but also as families and as communities.

Application: *Inclusive Christian schools are open to serving students with disabilities because they are fellow image bearers of God.*

All people, including those with disabilities, are created in God's image. Thus, all students, including those with disabilities, uniquely represent God in some way. This creative act of God bestowed a primary identity upon all people as glorious reflections of God. Christians fulfill this primary identity as God's image bearers—in Christ.

We reflect God's image both individually and collectively. Each student with a disability bears God's image and is worthy of consideration for enrollment and ongoing support in our schools. Our schools also bear an image collectively. The choices we ultimately make to include or exclude certain students will bear upon this image. Inclusive school communities are open to serving all students as image bearers and glorious reflections of God.

Pillar 2: God's Image Bearers—A Distorted Reflection

However, since humanity's fall described in Genesis 3, our ability to reflect God accurately has been fractured. As human persons, we still image Him, yet the reflection is now cast in distorted ways. For we have all been alienated from God through rebellion—our hearts have become bent to our own will and our purpose, distortedly focused on our own glory. At the same time, we experience differing elements of brokenness in every aspect of our personhood as a result of being born into—and living our lives in—a world impacted by the effects of the fall. We experience brokenness in our bodies, minds, intellect, emotions, and social relationships. Disability is simply a more *noticeable* form of the brokenness and difficulty that is *common* to the human condition. It is experienced both functionally (through bodies that do not work as we expect them to) and socially (through relationships that do not respect, support, and affirm as we need them to).

Application: *Inclusive Christian schools guard against reflecting the brokenness of the world by INcluding students with disabilities and EXcluding unbiblical values.*

The first pillar of disability theology calls Christian schools to strive for *inclusionary* practices that enroll and support students with disabilities. The second pillar calls Christian schools to also strive for *exclusionary* practices—but just not toward students. Your particular school distinctives should reflect the beauty of God and the diversity of His people while guarding against reflecting the brokenness of the world. In other words, your school should strive to create an inclusive learning community that is *in* the world but not *of* the world. Christian schools offer families a Christ-centered alternative to most other forms of schooling. While schools should be responsive to the pain and brokenness of the world, they should not reflect nor perpetuate it by excluding students with disabilities. Embracing students with disabilities is a commitment that can help ground biblical values and guard against ungodly ones.

Pillar 3: God's Promise to Remedy the Effects of the Fall

God never leaves us without hope. Even in the garden, after the fall, God proclaimed that a woman would bear a Seed who would crush Satan's head (Gen. 3:15), to overcome all alienation that separates us from God and each other—bringing restoration to the brokenness and difficulty experienced in this age.

Building on Genesis 3:15, Isaiah 53 predicted that when this Seed came he would have no beauty or majesty that we should desire him. He would be despised and rejected, a man of sorrows acquainted with the deepest grief. The One who would crush Satan's head would himself be crushed in order to redeem us from our sin and to heal our brokenness. He would be pierced for our transgressions and crushed for our iniquities.

Application: *Inclusive Christian schools should incubate and promote biblical faith that helps students know and trust God's wisdom and His ways.*

God's plans will not be thwarted. His promises are sure. While disability presents challenges to families and schools, they are not tragedies to be avoided but opportunities to embrace. God's ways are higher than our ability to fully understand. Proverbs 3:5-6 exhorts us to "Trust in the LORD with all your heart, and do not lean on your own understanding. In all your ways acknowledge him, and he will make straight your paths." God has a good purpose in mind when He brings students with disabilities to your school. The question is whether you will trust and obey in faith or not?

Just as the Fall has a remedy in God's Righteous One coming to crush all enemies, so too is God trustworthy to provide and equip you for everything to which He has called you and your school. School leaders are seldom fully equipped in advance to do what they are called to pursue. Doing it anyway is a mark of strong leadership. We take steps out in faith and work hard to make them successful, and often discover God has been working in advance to make those steps solid in His ways. Everyone in your school community—students,

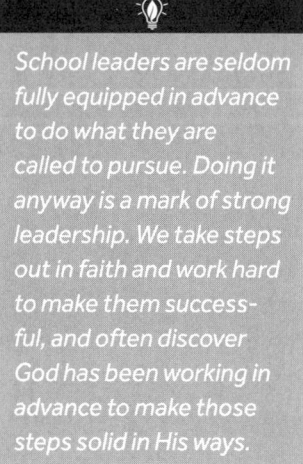

School leaders are seldom fully equipped in advance to do what they are called to pursue. Doing it anyway is a mark of strong leadership. We take steps out in faith and work hard to make them successful, and often discover God has been working in advance to make those steps solid in His ways.

staff, and families—all need to learn to trust God with the faith of Abraham who trusted and obeyed even though he did not have a full picture of where he was going. Like Abraham, we need to walk by faith in the good promises and pathways of God, even (and especially) when they are difficult.

Pillar 4: God's Remedy through the Messiah's Arrival

The Gospels tell of Jesus' life, death, resurrection, and ascension as the initial installment of God's promise of full restoration in His future return. In the testimony of the Apostles and Prophets, we see Jesus as the Messianic Seed who opened the door for complete salvation, including the "crippled, blind, and lame" (Luke 14:12–23). Moreover, all who invite in and embrace these individuals described as having various disabilities are promised a reward in the age to come (Luke 14:14).

Application: *Inclusive Christian schools exercise their faith by using existing resources and looking for ways God is leading to grow and build the school as a unique expression of Himself.*

The general education curriculum bears witness to various aspects of natural wisdom. God's Word bears witness to a higher wisdom. The Messiah's first coming decisively began restoring what was lost in the Fall. While the fullness of this kingdom is still *not yet*, there is still something possible in the *now*. The testimony of Jesus disrupts the natural order of things in service of restoring all people, and all creation, to God's holy purposes of bearing witness to His goodness and glory. Our curricula may be more or less explicit about studying the Bible, but how we respond to the vulnerable members of our community will instruct and model the wisdom of our curricula.

In our journeys toward becoming more inclusive schools, the best next step is to start with what we've already got—existing resources and staff—and identify areas where we want to grow. If we cannot yet afford new support staff, we can still provide additional training to existing staff. If we cannot yet enroll students with significant disabilities, we can still invest in strengthening individualized supports for instruction and assessment for current students who need them. Small steps can lead to bigger ones. Trusting God means relying on Him to provide in just the right time and in just the right ways for accomplishing everything to which He's called your school.

Pillar 5: God's Goodness and Sovereignty in the Face of Disability

In John 9—the story of Jesus' encounter with the man born blind—we see Jesus' most clear example of how the functional and social aspects of disability are reversed by the coming of God's kingdom. First, he corrects the disciples' misconceptions that the man born blind experienced this disability because of personal sin (misconceptions that had created heartbreaking social barriers for the man born blind). Instead, Jesus declares that "this happened that the works of God might be displayed in his life." The man's disability was made purposeful in the hands of a good, loving, and sovereign heavenly Father—working in the context of a broken world. Secondly, Jesus restored the man's vision—the function of his sight. This demonstration of God's power was an initial installment toward the full restoration of the brokenness of the fall. We see Jesus holding in tension human brokenness and difficulty with divine value and purpose. As Jesus's disciples, we are called to do the same.

Application: *Inclusive Christian schools pursue beauty (in all people and creation) amidst the brokenness that is common in this current age (i.e., before Jesus' return and the age to come).*

There is a tension between beauty and brokenness. All people are beautiful in that they represent God and His image in the world. Disability does not tarnish that image. Brokenness also characterizes all people—though, like Adam and Eve in the garden, we try to hide our own brokenness as much as possible. The Gospel, however, allows us to rest in truth that God accepts us in Jesus, despite all our brokenness—and helps us accept others in all their brokenness. This acceptance of others includes students with disabilities. While certain students may challenge the limits of our ability to accept others, it is a holy challenge with important consequences. Having eyes of faith to pursue and see the beauty amidst brokenness makes powerful declarations that God is both sovereign and good. Christian schools have a holy purpose to make these declarations by their culture of accepting and affirming the beauty of all students—even those with intense challenges or significant disabilities.

Pillar 6: God's Economy

In God's economy, human value is not measured by what we can or cannot do, but instead by Whose we are. When Moses hesitated to accept God's commission to deliver his people by citing a self-perceived limitation or disability, God responds by saying, "Who has made man's mouth? Who makes him mute, or deaf, or seeing, or blind? Is it not I, the LORD? Now therefore go, and I will be with your mouth and teach you what you shall speak" (Exod. 4:11–12). God sees no barriers to using those with disabilities to accomplish His purposes. Again, the apostle Paul declares that the seemingly weaker members

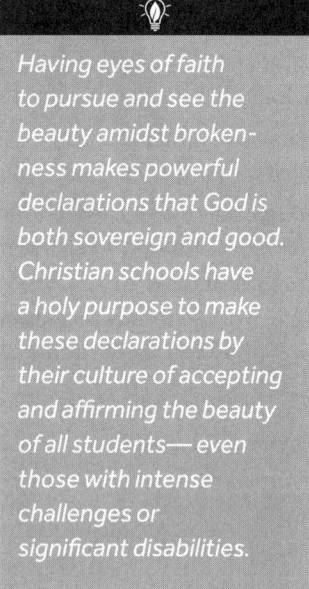

Having eyes of faith to pursue and see the beauty amidst brokenness makes powerful declarations that God is both sovereign and good. Christian schools have a holy purpose to make these declarations by their culture of accepting and affirming the beauty of all students— even those with intense challenges or significant disabilities.

of the believing community are indispensable and to be given double honor (1 Cor. 12:20-26). Furthermore, weakness is actually portrayed as a platform to perfect and display God's power (2 Cor. 12:9). Those perceived as weak and less worthy of praise by human standards are not only suitable—but at times they are uniquely gifted—for displaying God's glory and goodness.

Application: Inclusive Christian schools embrace and model God's economy by making room for human weakness so God's power can be more visible.

> *Those perceived as weak and less worthy of praise by human standards are not only suitable—but at times they are uniquely gifted—for displaying God's glory and goodness.*

Schools offer a place for students to gain important knowledge and skills for a successful life. But success can be defined in different ways. A successful life according to the standards of the world are not the same as the standards of God and His kingdom. Consider our schools' mission statements and the priorities they reflect. Is our commitment to strong academics framed within a larger biblical context? Are athletic opportunities, including ones involving rigorous competition, part of our schools' extracurricular programming? Character matters and God's economy makes room for students to learn that their human strength of mind and body are not the only valued traits. For example, Jesus modeled and taught about the strength required to serve others.

Furthermore, it takes strength to let your own weaknesses and needs be known by others. By acknowledging and embracing personal limitations—in those with and without disabilities—you make room for God to display His presence and power in and through your personal life and your collective school community. Investing your time, treasure, and talent in becoming a more inclusive Christian school can help everyone in your learning community recognize the inherent limitations of pursuing or boasting in academic prowess or athletic strength alone. Welcoming and walking with students with differing abilities goes a long way toward embodying the economy of God and His kingdom more than the values of secular society. Valuing human weakness to make God's strength more visible is an investment in God's economy.

Pillar 7: God's Law of Love

The apostle Paul also declares in 1 Corinthians 13 that if we give lip service without love to others—including the marginalized—we are nothing but sounding gongs. Furthermore, if we donate goods to feed them without love, we gain nothing. Love equalizes human brokenness. And God himself is love (1 John 4:8).

Love makes demands on how we treat other people. As finite creatures, human beings are all limited in various ways. Additionally, none of us are autonomous and completely self-sufficient. Moreover, what constitutes a "disability" and who has one can vary from culture to culture. When measured against some level of minimal or average performance or standing, we must acknowledge the arbitrariness of such standards. Conceptually, disability is an equalizer by focusing love's demands where they are needed most and reflect God's character best.

Disability equalizes us pragmatically and experientially as well. It is not partial to any race/ethnicity, religion, sex, age, or socioeconomic class. If we have not yet been touched by a disability (whether physical, intellectual, developmental, or neuro-atypical)—or by mental illness—we or one of our loved ones are likely to be impacted eventually.

Application: *Inclusive Christian schools prioritize loving God and others well so God's love can be more tangible and visible.*

God's economy also requires holy acts of human love. Jesus not only taught about God's love and modeled it through word and deed, Jesus also was—and is—love incarnate. Virtues such as love, however, need to be regularly taught, modeled, and practiced through curricular and extracurricular programming. Furthermore, opportunities for students and staff to interact in holy loving ways will go a long way to honor God and display something of His character. Students need opportunities to learn about and practice loving others who are different. Students with disabilities represent one type of difference that cuts across other dimensions of diversity such as race/ethnicity and socioeconomic status. Inclusive Christian schools prioritize this simple (in concept), yet difficult (in practice), requirement to love God and others with our whole heart, mind, and strength.

Pillar 8: God's People Respond

As God's people, what is our role in addressing disability? The church is to manifest God's love to a watching world (Eph. 3:10–11) as we live in countercultural ways that reflect the values of His kingdom. With Jesus as our Head, we constitute His Body. We are called to preserve unity in diversity (including diverse abilities), until we grow into the maturity and stature of Jesus (Eph. 4).

The unity of God's people does not depend upon human talent or intellect. It depends on our union with Jesus. This is a relational oneness in Messiah (who Himself is one with the Father) and with one another (John 17). Furthermore, as God has placed each part in the body just as He wanted (1 Cor. 12:18), so each has a divine purpose and gift that serves the body (1 Pet. 4:10). Indeed, God has "put the body together, giving greater honor to the less honorable so that there would be no division in the body, but that the members would have the same concern for each other so that if one member suffers, all the members suffer with it; if one member is honored, all the members rejoice with it" (1 Cor. 12:24–26, NIV).

While suffering in this age is unavoidable, God desires for all people to belong and flourish in community. While God does not promise to remove all sources of suffering in this age, He does promise to be with us and never leave us in our suffering. Furthermore, God often pours out His blessings upon His children through the loving words and deeds of others. Therefore, people of all abilities need one another for the unity, diversity, and growth in the perfect love of God, all for the glory of God.

Application: *As an extension and expression of the body of Christ, inclusive Christian schools cultivate interdependent community among students (and staff) of all abilities to learn and grow together in knowing and following Jesus.*

In American culture, we tend to overvalue independence and undervalue dependency. In contrast, the Bible presents a different recipe for human flourishing. Overvaluing personal achievement, autonomy, and self-reliance can undermine healthy dependence and relational intimacy with others. Rugged individualism may have helped build the United States, but when unchecked, it can also create a corrosive self-oriented and self-indulgent culture rather than foster a culture of honoring and loving others in all their weaknesses and needs. God's path of flourishing for individuals (with and without disabilities) and communities—including school communities—involves healthy and holy interdependence. This interdependence is described and depicted biblically as a relationally united community, that is committed and submitted to God.

Pillar 9: God's Ultimate Restoration of All Things in the Age to Come

The Seed predicted in Genesis 3:15 came into the world the

first time to crush the serpent's head and bring salvation to all who put their faith in Him (Rom. 10:11–13). Jesus, this King of the Jews and desire of all nations (Haggai 2:7), will come again to subject the enemy to final judgment. Under Messiah's reign there will be no more mourning, crying, or pain (Rev. 21:3–4). Together we look to His return. The Spirit and the Bride say, Come (Rev. 22:17)!

Application: *Inclusive Christian schools distinguish between primary outcomes, such as maturing disciples, and secondary outcomes, such as smarter students.*

Schools support students to learn and grow. The metrics of growth for a Christian school, however, must be measured with God's standards that have a different horizon line—a different plumb line. Supporting students to mature in godliness—which includes stewarding intellectual capacity—is a larger and more primary goal than merely helping students become smarter. Being and making disciples who are followers of Jesus who know God and make Him known is our primary mandate in the Great Commission, and we are called to obey the Great Commandment to love God and others in doing so. Inclusive Christian schools recognize that students with disabilities are not problems to avoid nor people with needs too heavy to carry in a learning community with limited resources. Students with disabilities are people created in the image of God and

> *Inclusive Christian schools recognize that students with disabilities are not problems to avoid nor people with needs too heavy to carry in a learning community with limited resources. Students with disabilities are people created in the image of God and in God's economy are essential members with gifts to share.*

in God's economy are essential members with gifts to share. These gifts become more easily received and recognized when our ultimate goals in God frame and shape the penultimate ones that are prized in secular schools.

Building and Growing Our Schools

Psalm 127:1 declares, "Unless the LORD builds the house, those who build it labor in vain." Christian schools should build on the solid foundation of God's Word with Jesus as the precious cornerstone. The nine pillars presented in this chapter offer solid principles from God's Word to help undergird and inspire our next steps toward serving students with disabilities.

Creating Communities of Belonging
Erik W. Carter, *Vanderbilt University*
Elizabeth Lucas Dombrowski, *All Belong*
Thomas L. Boehm, *Wheaton College*

Are our schools places of belonging for every student? This pressing question should be a point of regular reflection for every Christian school. Far too often, decisions about who does and does not belong are defined more by contemporary culture than by Christian values. Yet many Christian school mission statements locate education within a larger gospel framework and identify creating followers of Jesus as a central priority.

Consider for example your school's mission statement: *Does your vision include all God's children or only some? Does it apply to all image bearers or only those seen as having a particular range of abilities? Are students with disabilities part of your vision to develop followers of Jesus? Should a disability disqualify a student from such a holy calling?*

Creating a community of belonging for students of all abilities can reinforce your school's mission and create a radically biblical culture reflecting the heart of God, thereby impacting student learning, influencing well-being, and reflecting the Gospel call to unity and love. Yet this experience of belonging can be elusive for many children with disabilities. Too many families have stories about their child's schooling that begins or ends with exclusion. Too many children are missing out on the loving embrace of a Christian school community.

Through our ongoing work with individuals and families impacted by disability in schools, churches, and

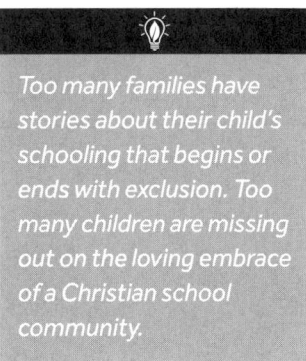

Too many families have stories about their child's schooling that begins or ends with exclusion. Too many children are missing out on the loving embrace of a Christian school community.

communities, we often ask questions about their experiences of inclusion and belonging, such as, *What is it that contributes to a sense of belonging for you? What do people say and do that assure you that you truly do belong?* Although the answers they share are always personal, we have heard some recurring themes that resonate for many people. In one of our recent studies, we heard that belonging is experienced when children with disabilities are *present, invited, welcomed, known, accepted, supported, cared for, befriended, needed,* and *loved* (Carter, Biggs and Boehm 2016). In this chapter we present an overview of these ten dimensions of belonging, along with why they matter for children with disabilities and what schools might do to foster deeper belonging for all students. Each section ends with a few questions to spur reflection on the extent to which each dimension of belonging is experienced in your school.

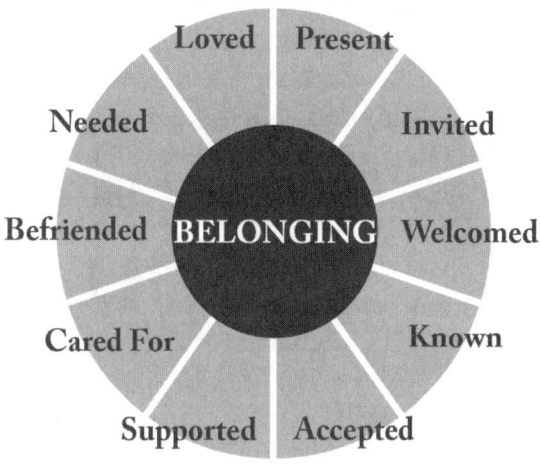

Ten Dimensions of Belonging

"I Am Present"

Far too many families who desire a strong Christian education still struggle to find a school that will embrace their children with disabilities. Likewise, far too many Christian schools struggle to include students with disabilities across the entire array of educational and social opportunities they offer. Yet belonging is usually built upon a foundation of shared experiences and encounters over time. As children spend time with their peers in and beyond the classroom, opportunities to be known, accepted, supported, befriended, needed, and loved become all the more available. After all, it is hard to feel like you really belong within a school in which you are never—or are only peripherally—a part. Belonging begins with presence. In other words, students with disabilities should be enrolled in every Christian school and take part in all that school has to offer.

Nearly one in seven children—about 15 percent—has a disability that somehow impacts their learning or relationships (Hussar et al. 2020). For some students, this impact may be quite substantial and readily apparent. For other students, their needs may be much less visible or evident in only certain areas. What would a peek into your classrooms, cafeterias, courtyards, and clubs say about the presence of students with disabilities throughout your school? If their absence is more common than their presence, reflect on what might be hindering the access and involvement of students with disabilities. What are some barriers that stand in the way of presence (e.g., physical accessibility, financial resources, social acceptance)? What changes might be needed to deepen the journey of belonging by increasing the presence of students with disabilities in your school?

It is important, too, to examine your community's understandings of disability. Disability can take many forms, including physical, intellectual, developmental, learning, or emotional. Although we need to recognize the meaning that a disability label confers, it is also crucial to remember that God's people are incredibly complex and unique. If your school community has a narrow picture of who comes to mind when you think about serving students with disabilities (for example, as serving just students with ADHD), consider how you might broaden this commitment. *Questions to consider:*

- *How many students with disabilities are enrolled in your school?*

- *To what degree are they involved in the breadth of academic and extracurricular activities you offer?*

- *Are they participating right alongside their schoolmates without disabilities?*

"I Am Invited"

The antidote to absence is an active invitation. The experience of being sought out sends a powerful message to children with disabilities and their families, namely, "*We want you here. We need your presence. It would just not be the same here without you.*" Personal invitations go a long way toward quelling the uncertainty parents may feel as they wonder whether there truly is a place for their child in your school. In reality, such invitations remain much too rare within contemporary society. While it certainly speaks volumes when Christian schools are at the forefront of educational inclusion in their community, it also speaks volumes when they are not.

One such family recently moved from a school district where they were constantly fighting for inclusion to a city that had a number of inclusive Christian schools. They recounted that their new principal "actively pursued our family. They wanted [our son] at their school, and reassured us that they have been doing inclusion for a very long time." The contrast was striking in the school's demonstration of faithfulness.

The posture of Christian schools in this area should be proactive, not passive. This begins by asking who might be missing from your school. Are you pursuing the enrollment of children with Down syndrome, learning disabilities, physical disabilities, autism spectrum disorder, intellectual disability, emotional challenges, or other disabilities? Consider where and how you might extend new invitations throughout your local community so that families learn of your desire to serve their children. Often, legacy or highly invested families may assume that a student with disabilities must attend somewhere else; as a starting point, reach out to them intentionally with your desire to enroll whole families.

Review your school's website, print materials, and social media to ensure they clearly communicate your school's commitment to welcoming and supporting students with disabilities. Likewise, invitations should also abound for students with disabilities who are already members of your school—invitations to attend birthday parties, join extracurricular groups, assume leadership responsibilities, and be part of everyday school activities. Everyone has a gift to share. When invitations are explicitly extended to those with a variety of abilities, the journey toward belonging for all is enhanced. *Questions to consider:*

> Everyone has a gift to share. When invitations are explicitly extended to those with a variety of abilities, the journey toward belonging for all is enhanced.

- *Does your school actively encourage applications from students with disabilities? Are you recruiting entire families or only certain children?*

- *Are students with disabilities and available supports referenced in marketing materials?*

- *Are students with disabilities treated as equal and contributing members of the community?*

- *Are staff inviting the involvement of students with disabilities in all school activities?*

"I Am Welcomed"

When others delight in your presence, you feel at home. And when you are overlooked or ignored, you feel out of place. The posture with which children with disabilities are welcomed each day at school also impacts their sense of belonging. The hospitality they encounter from teachers in their classes and the eagerness with which they are greeted by peers assures them they have a real place within the school community. For many children with disabilities, however, there is no assurance they will experience a warm reception when they arrive. This should never be the case in Christian schools.

This sense of being welcomed is often communicated through the ordinary and everyday gestures of both peers and staff. Welcoming students with disabilities might include greeting them by name, finding out more about them, drawing them into conversations with others, asking about their week, supporting their involvement in class activities, sitting together at lunch, remembering important events in their lives, inviting them to other school events, and checking in when they are absent. Uncertainty about what to do or say (or not do or say) can sometimes make peers reluctant to interact with students with more significant disabilities. It is here where providing information, guidance, or modeling can be especially helpful. This can include showing peers what it looks like to use respectful language, to converse with students who experience complex communication challenges, or to work collaboratively with someone whose support needs are more extensive. All Belong (https://allbelong.org) provides a framework for creating plans for students, peers, parents/teachers, and the environment. When efforts are made to extend welcome to all students, regardless of ability, the journey toward belonging for all is meaningfully advanced. *Questions to consider:*

- *How eager and well-prepared are teachers to include students with disabilities in their classes?*
- *To what extent are students with and without disabilities interacting with one another?*
- *Are students with disabilities absolutely excited to come to your school each day?*

"I Am Known"

When students with disabilities have a presence throughout their school and are welcomed well, other people come to know them as children of God. As the refrain in the theme song of the old *Cheers* sitcom observes, "we all want to go where everybody knows our name." School is no different. Yet children with disabilities can sometimes feel like strangers in their own school. When students with disabilities spend most of their school day in separate classrooms or are always on the periphery of school activities, their opportunities to develop relationships with other students and staff throughout the entire school becomes much more limited. Moreover, the labels we as educators so often use to categorize students (e.g., learning disabilities, intellectual disability, autism spectrum disorder) can inadvertently shape *how* children are known—by their struggles rather than by their strengths, and by their challenges rather than by their contributions. Each of these ways of being known can hinder belonging.

Christian schools should be learning communities in which children with disabilities are seen as unique individuals who are created by God and endowed with inestimable worth. School leaders should strive to discover the gifts, talents, strengths, stories, passions, and positive qualities of each student they serve. They should view them through a Christlike lens that interprets behaviors in new and affirming ways. And they should find ways of fostering connections among students with and without disabilities that transform them from strangers to friends. Effectively modeling these efforts by school leaders will have myriad impacts on how peers relate to each other. When children with disabilities are known personally and deeply by others in these ways, they feel like they belong, and a school culture of belonging is enhanced for all.

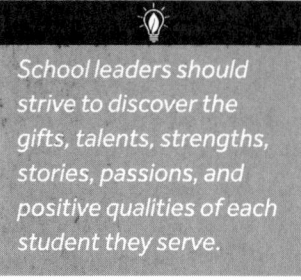

School leaders should strive to discover the gifts, talents, strengths, stories, passions, and positive qualities of each student they serve.

Questions to consider:

- *How well are children with disabilities known by others in your school?*
- *Are they seen as having strengths and gifts worth encountering and knowing?*
- *Do the labels you use to describe students present a portrait of strengths or deficits?*

"I Am Accepted"

Views about disability and inclusion have improved dramatically with each generation. But stigma, stereotypes, low expectations, and exclusion are still evident in so many communities across the country and around the world. Views about disability are what so often stand in the way of true belonging. Scot Danforth (2014) summarizes this approach well when he writes: "Students with disabilities receiving instruction in general education classrooms might be viewed as having trapdoors beneath their desks. At any moment, the educators can pull the lever. The door flops open, and the student drops down a shaft leading to a segregated special education setting" (43).

In contrast, students with disabilities should be assured they are welcomed without condition and embraced for all of who they are.

Friendships that are not contingent on abilities or accomplishments are essential. Students with learning differences need not earn their place at the table, nor must they meet some prevailing standard to be full-fledged members of the community. They simply and already belong, on the basis of having the same heavenly Father and being present in an earthly community united by the Christian school mission.

The moral imperative for Christian schools to foster a culture of acceptance is even greater when placed within the gospel message. Living this out may involve sharing accurate information about the capabilities and contributions of individuals with disabilities. It could entail hosting activities that raise awareness or increase understanding. It should involve modeling positive interactions, using affirming language, and holding high expectations. But acceptance is most likely to emerge when students with and without disabilities have positive interactions together over time. Attitudes are most likely to change because of ongoing personal encounters rather than merely through informational learning along the way. The informational becomes transformational when it is relational. Belonging depends on the security of being accepted among real relationships within a school's learning community of students and staff. *Questions to consider:*

- *What is the reaction of staff and students toward disability in your school?*

> Acceptance is most likely to emerge when students with and without disabilities have positive interactions together over time. Attitudes are most likely to change because of ongoing personal encounters rather than merely through informational learning along the way. The informational becomes transformational when it is relational.

- *Are children with disabilities truly welcomed without condition?*

- *Are we taking active steps to promote awareness and acceptance in our school?*

"I Am Supported"

Children with disabilities often need additional support to participate fully in the life of their school. This might include receiving academic assistance in certain classes, social supports during non-instructional times, or behavioral supports across the school day. For some students, this support will be modest or episodic, but for others it may be more substantial or ongoing. The provision of individualized support is a tangible demonstration of a school's commitment to students' educational flourishing and clearly communicates a desire for their presence. The absence of this support often leads to exclusion or limits meaningful participation.

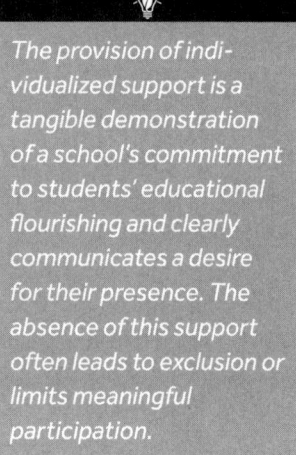

The provision of individualized support is a tangible demonstration of a school's commitment to students' educational flourishing and clearly communicates a desire for their presence. The absence of this support often leads to exclusion or limits meaningful participation.

Inclusion of students with a variety of abilities must be seen as an integral part of multi-tiered systems of support and response-to-intervention (these systems are described in depth in Chapter 7). Taking responsibility for student learning and success is a testimony of value to all families, regardless of their children's level of ability. Students' needs change over time, and your school's responses to those ever-changing needs can either build or undermine parent confidence that you are committed to this journey together.

Schools dedicated to belonging see the delivery of individualized supports as a core commitment, not as an optional endeavor. They use person-centered planning approaches to decide which supports might be most beneficial for each child. They build the capacity of all staff to support a diversity of students well in their classes and programs. They encourage peers to serve as natural supports to their schoolmates who need extra help. And they regularly revisit these supports to ensure they are continuing to work well for each student. Supporting each student well fosters and deepens a culture of belonging for all. *Questions to consider:*

- *Is our planning truly individualized and always person-guided?*

- *Are we seeking input from families, students, staff, and others on needed supports?*

- *Are we equipping teachers, support staff, and peers to provide strong supports?*

"I Am Cared For"

Effective schools focus on much more than academic learning. They also strive to care for the breadth of social, emotional, physical, and spiritual needs children experience each day. This deep concern for the overall well-being of students is equally important for children with disabilities. This care and concern becomes evident when educators notice the needs of students and find ways to address them. Indeed, parents greatly value schools known for having nurturing and supportive environments (Hunt and Van Pelt 2019).

The ordinary ways in which schools care for their students should also be extended to those who have disabilities. These ordinary expressions of care may include watching for students who need an invitation or a plan in order to participate in recess. Yet there may be additional needs the students bring to school each day that may require additional expressions of care. For example, peers can be taught to understand the warning signs of emotional distress as well as strategies that might calm a fellow student. Collectively, these expressions of care contribute to a deeper sense of belonging. In some cases, demonstrating these expressions of care for one student with disabilities can impact students without disabilities just as deeply. As the adults in the room, our teaching of the "unwritten" curriculum is just as impactful as the curriculum we intend to teach. For Christian schools, then, social-emotional learning must be built into the curriculum by design in order to foster spiritual growth. *Questions to consider:*

- *Are we adopting a holistic view of care?*
- *Is our school considered to be a supportive and nurturing community?*
- *Are we addressing needs of students and families that extend beyond the school day?*

"I Am Befriended"

We were created for community. Belonging is experienced best through relationships. In most schools, children with disabilities have no shortage of relationships with adults (e.g., teachers, educational assistants, related service providers, nurses, counselors, and other professionals). But their relationships with peers may have the strongest influence on their sense of belonging within the school. Friendships are central to belonging. The presence of friends can be enriching; their absence can be wounding. Yet study after study finds that friendships can be few or fleeting for so many children with disabilities (Carter 2018). Being together in the same school does not automatically lead to actual friendships, much less an abundance of them.

To build belonging, peer relationships and friendships should be prioritized right alongside addressing academic rigor. Teachers should create regular opportunities for collaborative learning and shared activities for students with and without disabilities within their classrooms. They should use peer-mediated support models that invite, equip, and assist peers to provide some of the support their schoolmates with disabilities might need (Ziegler et al 2020). This may involve the creation of a "Circle of Friends" or other peer network that provides ways for students to meet each other and develop new skills.

Special educators and general classroom teachers can support involvement in inclusive extracurricular activities through which students with and without disabilities can connect around common interests. When students with and without disabilities have regular, well-supported opportunities to connect with one another in this way, friendships are likely to emerge. A journey toward becoming a community of belonging flourishes when a culture of care for every student kindles friendships more easily. *Questions to consider:*

- *Do students with and without disabilities have regular opportunities to interact within and beyond the classroom?*

- *Are we active and intentional in fostering positive relationships among the students we serve?*

- *Are the friendship networks of students with disabilities rich and satisfying for all involved?*

"I Am Needed"

Everyone wants to feel needed. We hope to be recognized as having gifts and making contributions that enrich and enliven the entire community. We want some assurance that our presence matters and makes some meaningful difference in the lives of others. Paul's portrait of the church is a declaration that every person is utterly indispensable within the body (1 Cor. 12:12-31). Yet it is still quite rare for children with disabilities to be seen as the bearers of gifts, abilities, faith, and friendship that are needed in our schools. We focus almost exclusively instead on meeting their needs—and in doing so, inadvertently overlook the ways in which they might play a role in meeting the needs of others. True friends are missed when they are absent because they bring something meaningful to contribute to the relationship.

Christian schools should be a place where all students have friends and enjoy being the subjects of relationships rather than merely the objects of programming. They should be learning communities where the gifts of children with disabilities are anticipated and sought after. Teachers should take steps to discover their students' positive qualities and special talents, while also looking for places where each can be shared with others. They should also identify valued roles for students with disabilities throughout the school, such as having leadership responsibilities in a classroom or project, playing a role on a team, meeting needs in their community, participating in high-status activities, or contributing in any number of other ways. Each creates opportunities for students with disabilities to serve others, rather than remaining only on the receiving end of service. Being needed for one's unique contribution, and missed when one is absent, engenders a deeper sense of belonging.

There is a vulnerability in recognizing our need for others who we perceive to be unlike ourselves. But that is an expected part of creating communities of belonging. An attitude of inclusion expects such discomfort. As Kevin Timpe (2018) exhorts, "We need to stop expecting everyone to engage on terms that make us, not them, comfortable" (91). Likewise, a high school senior reflecting on their experience with inclusion noted, "You learn the most from the people you're least like. To learn how different people see the world is eye opening" (Barkley 2019). We can remember that time and time again in the Gospels, Jesus makes everyone uncomfortable. *Questions to consider:*

- *Do we strive to discover the gifts, talents, passions, and contributions of every student?*
- *Are students with disabilities participating in visible ways to engage, serve, and even lead others?*
- *Are they missed by others when they not there?*

"I Am Loved"

We are called to be a people who love lavishly. Likewise, we are also a people who need to be loved unconditionally. Above all things, Christian schools should abound in love. Such love compels us to invite, welcome, know, accept, support, care for, befriend, and need children with and without disabilities. And in doing so, our love for one another only grows deeper. Like anyone else, children with disabilities yearn to be part of a school community where they can love and be loved. It is in such a community that belonging is most likely to be experienced.

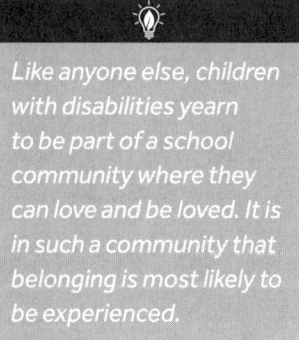

Like anyone else, children with disabilities yearn to be part of a school community where they can love and be loved. It is in such a community that belonging is most likely to be experienced.

In accomplishing a Christian school mission, this love should not be mistaken for permissiveness or offered in lieu of meaningful support. It must be combined with the other aspects of belonging, with a love based on knowing who the child is and a belief that every student has a sacred future ahead. Students must be provided with the supports and skills they need in order to add their meaningful presence to our faith communities. *Questions to consider:*

- *Are we actively proclaiming and pursuing the priority of love as being central to our school mission?*
- *Do students with disabilities at our school feel lavishly loved—by adults as well as peers?*
- *What supports might our team need in order to refill their own reservoirs and pour love into students?*

Moving Forward as a School

A first step toward inclusion and belonging in your school is making a firm commitment to create and nurture a community of belonging. Additionally, this commitment is better thought of as a journey than as a one-time endeavor. This journey deeper into belonging is best walked together, in partnership with parents, donors, board members, teachers, administrators, and students. Everyone will need to work together to grow in communication, collaboration, and collective problem solving. Take the time necessary to help everyone understand your commitment to students with diverse abilities and help foster unity around this commitment. Consider ways you might introduce the overall framework of belonging into professional development and school improvement plans.

Engaging the Christian school community with these ten dimensions of belonging can be rich and rewarding. As you move forward in your commitment, however, not everyone will share your enthusiasm. One proactive administrator writes a letter to parents at the beginning of each school year, explaining the school's mission and its implications for serving students of all abilities (Barkley 2017).

Successfully inclusive schools proactively address and anticipate potential behavior or social challenges that may arise—no community is perfect, after all. Although no school will be free from challenges or complexities, the commitment to pursuing a community of belonging for all will speak volumes and help make your values more visible.

These ten dimensions of belonging may resonate with different people in different ways. This is likely because the power of this model is that it is more descriptive of human needs rather than special needs or unique needs of people with disabilities. *Everyone* desires to belong within a community where they are known and valued. Committing and moving deeper into acceptance, love, and belonging can help every student experience and learn about the character of God and grow to be more like Him.

Your school mission embodies the vision God has given to your school. It is important to consider how this vision intentionally applies to students with diverse abilities. Do you apply this vision by recognizing and honoring the image of God in every person? By intentionally serving all God's children, including those with disabilities, your school will send the clear message that regardless of any level of ability, we all belong in Christ.

A Review of the Research on Inclusive Christian Education

Kate E. Strater, *Calvin University*

In the United States, approximately 4.9 million children attend private schools, with 78 percent of that number attending private, faith-based schools (Broughman and Pugh 2019). Approximately 2.5 percent of children attending any private school have been identified as children with disabilities (Broughman and Pugh 2019) compared to 14 percent enrollment of students with disabilities in public schools (National Center for Education Statistics 2019). Lane and Jones (2015a), in their survey of 240 faith-based schools from preschool through grade 12, found that the proportion of students with disabilities served in faith-based schools can vary widely from 1 percent to close to 18 percent. Burke and Griffin (2016), in their case studies of enrollment practices, found that students with developmental disabilities or who need extensive supports are rarely served within the faith-based school community.

As Christian educators, we are called to embrace and uphold all members of the body of Christ. With the goal of supporting ongoing work toward inclusivity for students with disabilities in Christian schools, this chapter describes the research and literature related to inclusive Christian education and identifies directions for future research. Mitchell (2015) described inclusive education for children with disabilities as a multifaceted concept that includes vision; leadership; acceptance; placement; teaching, curriculum, and assessment; access; support; and resources. While this list of discrete features does not capture fully the effort, spirit, and culture necessary for embracing the unique talents of individual learners (Lai and Zhang 2014), it provides a helpful organizational structure for describing the current practices of inclusion in Christian schools.

Vision for Inclusion

Christian schools implementing inclusion often follow denominational traditions and Scripture recognizing all people as members of the body of Christ and a responsibility to care for one another, with each child identified as a bearer of the image of God. It moves beyond the individualized nature of access and service provision toward communal value of the unique contribution of each member (Hoeksema 2007; Anderson 2011). Pirner (2015) states, "The goal here is the community, the ideal of wholeness and completeness refers to the social body instead of the individual" (236). Carlson (2014), making a moral case for inclusive school practices, states, "to give to each what is needed to live decently and to flourish, beyond including material goods to also include services such as education, is justified" (73).

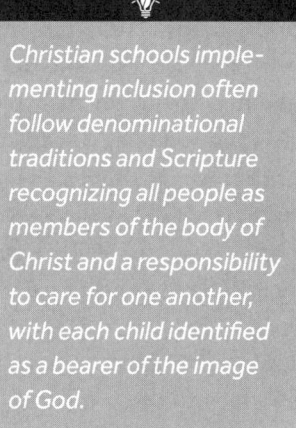

Christian schools implementing inclusion often follow denominational traditions and Scripture recognizing all people as members of the body of Christ and a responsibility to care for one another, with each child identified as a bearer of the image of God.

Each Christian school community determines how this vision for inclusive education is carried out through the interpretation of Scripture and its impact on the development of inclusive school practices (Contreras 2013). Literature addressing and describing a vision for inclusive Christian education is by far the most extensive compared to the other areas within Mitchell's framework. Vision has been described in terms of a communal commitment to biblical understandings of hospitality, justice, reconciliation, mutuality, and interdependence (Anderson 2003, 2006a, 2010, 2011).

Hospitality is one lens through which inclusive educational communities can be envisioned to promote human flourishing in all who bear God's image. Teachers and school leaders share a Christ-centered commitment to meet each student with a posture of hospitality

(Contreras 2013; DeFiore 2006; Hoeksema 2007; Lane, Kinnison and Ellard 2019; Long and Schuttloffel 2006; Mercer 2015; Oosterhuis, 2002; Paxton-Buursma 2007; Van Dyk 2010). Hospitable teachers break down barriers; build bridges; welcome all students; respond to learners with support and instruction; foster friendships; encourage reciprocity between community members; grow their own understanding of the learner; provide safety, security, emotional support, and opportunities for student empowerment; and commit to providing unconditional positive regard for all students in the classroom (Anderson 2011). Hospitable schools see that some students have been disadvantaged by the way traditional schools have responded to them and grow their community centered around the removal of structural and attitudinal barriers that cause stigmatization and isolation (Hoeksema 2007). Hospitable schools celebrate the gifts and talents of their community members and prioritize flourishing of all students within their walls.

In addition to hospitality, within the literature describing vision, writers also address the relationship between *biblical justice, reconciliation, mutuality,* and *shalom*. Hoeksema (2007) writes, "Living shalom means that students will learn to take action against injustices that affect their neighbor as quickly as they do when injustices affect themselves. Shalom exists when students comprehend how mutually interconnected people are and recognize the reciprocity that exists in relationships between people who have different constellations of capacity and incapacity" (4). The vision for inclusive Christian education connects students with disability to their peers in mutually beneficial and interdependent relationships. Furthermore, Anderson (2010) describes an understanding of biblical justice and reconciliation as a cornerstone for building truly inclusive educational communities, "But community does not mean uniformity. The Bible is clear in teaching that each person is an individual. Although all are created as God's image, each is uniquely designed, gifted, and purposed" (346). Without interconnectedness and pervasive actions of community, inclusive programming has the potential to fall short in establishing the interdependence and belonging of all community members (Anderson 2006b).

Inclusion Practices

One outcome of inclusive education is the connection of each student to the school community, culture, and organization (Pudlas 2004). Inclusive education is not a "place" but rather an approach to the development of practices and relationships necessary for all students to experience the responsibilities and benefits of community membership, academic challenge, social reciprocity, and personal growth that is a result of full participation in an academic and social school community. Inclusion can be described as a philosophy or atmosphere where all belong (Taylor 2005). This philosophy, however, must translate into educational practice if it is to be considered authentically held within a given school community. Educational practices that are shaped by an inclusion philosophy include teaching, curriculum, and assessment.

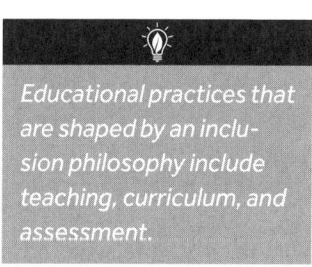

Educational practices that are shaped by an inclusion philosophy include teaching, curriculum, and assessment.

Little attention has been focused on identifying or evaluating pedagogical practices within schools engaging in Christian inclusive education. Paxton-Buursma (2007) suggested a pedagogical method for developing in-depth learner profiles, identifying curricular content responsive to these profiles, and making instructional decisions based on the concepts of differentiation, Universal Design for Learning (UDL), and socio-constructivist learning theories. This provides a potential framework for pedagogy in inclusive Christian education classrooms. Without any available research describing or evaluating this process in a Christian context, the remainder of this section describes the rationale for curricular choices, a case study describing instructional practices in one Christian school, and instructional needs identified in the literature.

According to Lane, Kinnison, and Ellard (2019), Christian schools practicing inclusive education share a common outlook that nurturing relationships is essential for modeling the value of all God's children, demonstrating love for neighbor, and developing character. All pedagogies flow from this theological understanding. Therefore, children with disabilities enrolled in inclusive Christian schools are educated alongside their peers for the majority of their day and are afforded opportunities to participate fully in extracurricular activities. Peer partners may be engaged to work alongside students with disabilities. Lesson planning is differentiated, use of person-first language is taught, and the value and impact of inclusion on the lives of all students is recognized (Lane, Kinnison and Ellard 2019). Additionally, Burke and Griffin (2016) outlined a hospitable program structure that includes collaborative enrollment policies, supported academic programming, extensive social programming, and inter-agency transition planning.

Cappiello (2013) described how one Christian high school served students with emotional and behavioral disabilities, and identified the following instructional strategies as instrumental in supporting students to meet graduation requirements: 1) varied instructional methods responsive to learner profile; 2) customized curriculum based on learner profile and assessment; 3) small teacher-to-student ratio; 4) use of assistive technology; 5) frequent assessment; 6) regular positive feedback; 7) daily character lessons utilizing biblical principles; 8) relationship-building between teachers, administrators, students, and families; and 9) a flexible school schedule.

Inclusion Models

Research and literature addressing support models for inclusive Christian education can be described as growing. Support for Christian school implementation of inclusive and/or special education services generally adheres to two approaches: 1) consultation services to support school- or system-wide commitment to inclusive practice and organizational change (Scanlan 2009a); and/or 2) additional services for individual students enrolled in an existing general education program, either provided in-house by trained professionals in the individual school or through collaboration with the local public school district. The first approach has the potential to greatly increase the inclusion of students with disabilities in the general education classroom community, while the second approach remains reliant on services delivered outside of the regular education classroom, potentially limiting time in the general education setting, engagement in community-building, and opportunity for education alongside same-age peers.

Scanlan (2009a) described the *learning consultant model* as an integrated and comprehensive approach responsive to learners: "It emphasizes inclusive service delivery, prevention of student failure, and tiered interventions to meet the needs of students who struggle, including those who have diagnosed disabilities and those who may be considered at risk for disabilities" (543). The learning consultant model has the potential to build classroom contexts responsive to learner profiles, focus on community-building, and support mutuality. At the center of this model is comprehensive service delivered at the school and classroom level; collegial relationships and collaborative planning between general educators and a special educator serving in the role of consultant; school culture development; provision of accessible instruction for all students in the regular classroom; and professional learning and capacity-building among staff (Taylor 2005; Scanlan 2009b). Burke and Griffin (2016) described two case studies where schools practicing inclusive Christian education implemented a continuum of special and inclusive educational services. All enrolled students with disabilities attended classes with their same-age peers, engaged in social programming, and participated in extracurricular activities. Individualized services to support academic, social, spiritual, and functional development were also offered with certified special education teachers responsive to the needs of individual students.

The *additional services model* relies on the provision of additional services to students enrolled in existing general education classrooms, without an articulated focus on contextual responsiveness, mutuality, interdependence, and community. For this reason, this model has the potential to run counter to the vision for inclusive Christian education, even if academic and skills-based outcomes of such a model are positive. One example of this model is the National Institute for Learning Development (NILD), which provides a variety of services to students in Christian schools including individual therapy, teacher training, and in-school interventions (NILD 2020). A 2017 phenomenological study of the experiences of ten parents of children with learning differences enrolled in an NILD program in five Christian elementary and secondary schools indicated positive parent perception of their child's academic success in school. The primary means of service delivery was the children's enrollment in an NILD Educational Therapy program while being enrolled in a general education classroom. Students received educational therapy through pull-out services and accommodations and modifications coordinated by the NILD therapist (Bayer 2017).

Public school collaboration is likewise an example of additional services being provided to students at private Christian schools. In a 2017 survey of 329 faith-based schools, 53.2 percent reported serving students with disabilities without teachers credentialed in the field of special education (Lane 2017). Public school administrators are mandated through the IDEA to collaborate with administrators of faith-based schools to provide special education and related services to students enrolled in private school programs (Osborne, DiMattia and Russo 1998; Russo, Cattaro and Osborne 1999;

Eigenbrood 2005, 2010; Russo et al. 2011). IDEA requirements for public and private school collaboration include: 1) public schools must engage in activities to identify all children with disabilities whether they are enrolled in public or private school; 2) public schools must spend a proportionate amount of IDEA Part B funds on behalf of students with disabilities enrolled in private schools; 3) public schools must make special education and related services available to students with disabilities enrolled in private schools as a group; and 4) public schools must decide, in consultation with personnel of faith-based schools, which services will be provided and where they will be delivered (Eigenbrood 2010). In a survey of 240 faith-based schools in the United States, 65.2 percent reported a collaborative relationship with their local public schools (Lane and Jones 2015b). While public school collaboration can increase much-needed access to resources for faith-based schools providing services to students with disabilities, it is important to keep in mind whether and how such services could be leveraged while at the same time promoting an inclusive educational experience in Christian schools.

Personnel and Leadership

Eigenbrood (2005) recommended that faith-based school administrators require teachers in special and inclusive education programs to have *training and licensure* similar to that required of special educators in public schools. The purpose is to ensure that teachers are trained in instructional planning and implementation of evidence-based practices. This leaves room for growth in the training and development of Christian educators serving students with disabilities. In addition to the training and licensure of teachers for instructional excellence, schools could extend training requirements to include facilitation and support of the meaningful participation of each student in their school community (Stegink 2010). Case study research describes implementation of programs and supports designed to create opportunities to expand teaching to the social inclusion and active participation of students with disabilities in the life of the school (Burke and Griffin 2016).

Professional learning and development is another key component to the implementation of school- or system-wide inclusive practice. Currently, only limited data describing the professional learning and qualifications of teachers serving students with disabilities is available (Lane and Jones 2014). Cunningham et al. (2017) evaluated a system-wide professional development approach instituted in Catholic schools to prepare regular education teachers for providing effective support to students with moderate disabilities. The program centered on implementation of UDL across all classrooms, external experts to support professional learning of the concepts of UDL, and job-embedded coaches to support ongoing implementation. The researchers found that teachers who fully engaged in the professional learning experience saw improved student engagement and access to the curriculum for all students in their classes, including recently enrolled students with moderate disabilities. Additional support for school- or system-wide professional learning is supported by a case study conducted by Lane (2011) that focused solely on special education providers. This approach was less effective for producing school-wide change and identified the need for policy, procedures, and support spearheaded by school leadership.

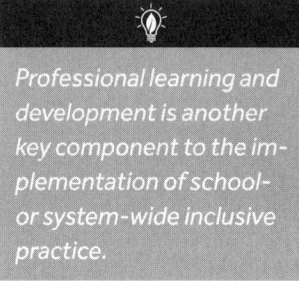
Professional learning and development is another key component to the implementation of school- or system-wide inclusive practice.

In addition to that for teaching staff, the literature addressing *leadership practices* in inclusive Christian education can be described as growing. Several studies and papers indicate the importance of administrator embrace of the vision and mission for inclusive and hospitable education; clear communication of the vision with all teachers, stakeholders, and community members; articulation of policy and procedure; and support for implementers (Taylor 2005; Scanlan 2009b; Lane 2011; Poon-McBrayer and Wong 2013; Sergeant and Berkner 2015; Lane, Kennison and Ellard 2019). Furthermore, collegial and trusting relationships between administrators and teachers are identified as vital for creating cultural shifts needed for full implementation of inclusive education (Scanlan 2009b; Poon-McBrayer and Wong 2013).

Cookson and Smith (2011) identified the importance of school leaders in establishing the vision and mission for inclusive Christian education. School leaders, convicted of biblical understanding of inclusion in the body of Christ, committed themselves to financial policies making it possible to include all students in a Christian school community, addressed opposition from faculty, and worked cooperatively with all parents and families. As a result of this sustained work, school leaders observed benefits to their school communities in the form of mutuality, care, and understanding within the student body.

> School leaders, convicted of biblical understanding of inclusion in the body of Christ, committed themselves to financial policies making it possible to include all students in a Christian school community, addressed opposition from faculty, and worked cooperatively with all parents and families.

Funding

Contreras (2013) found that primary barriers to inclusive Christian education "reside in the tension between commodity versus community, and between individualism versus family" (103). This tension is manifested in a school- or system-wide approach to resource development either as an understanding of inclusive education services as an additional cost or as a primary component of a school budget (Craig 2010). While collaborating with the local public schools provides some access to funding, professional development, services, and human resources (Eigenbrood 2005, 2010), the need for a school- or system-wide approach to developing and assigning resources remains. Three barriers to the enrollment of students with disabilities in inclusive Christian education include: 1) limited financial resources to implement adequate support systems for students (DeFiore 2006; Stymeist and Ramirez 2010; Mercer 2015; Burke and Griffin 2016); 2) lack of a clear framework, oversight, or policy for the planning, implementation, resource development, and coordination of individual school efforts toward inclusive Christian education (Eigenbrood 2005; Craig 2010; Burke and Griffin 2016); and 3) limited access to information about effective inclusive education models (Burke and Griffin 2016).

Burke and Griffin (2016) describe two case examples of funding models in use in inclusive education programs. In the first model, families of children with disabilities pay $200 in additional tuition, and the remaining costs are funded through allocation of funds from fundraising events, grants, and support from local foundations. The second model utilizes an equitable tuition structure, drawing funds from an annual fundraising event, individual donors, and funds allocated to students attending private schools through the Individuals with Disabilities Education Act (IDEA). An equitable tuition model should be considered a standard feature for inclusive Christian education, as it is foundational for building a community of mutuality and eliminating disability-related stigma (Hoeksema 2007). [Funding approaches for inclusion in Christian schools will be addressed in Chapter 8.]

The Future of Research and Practice

To grow understanding of the implementation of inclusive Christian education and meet the calling for pervasive inclusivity, more research is needed. This chapter presents a review of the research and literature addressing various aspects of inclusive Christian education; however, now is the time to engage in research that directly impacts program expansion and improvement. Three themes emerged indicating potential research priorities:

- Leadership practices have been identified by teachers as key to implementing and sustaining inclusive Christian education (Taylor 2005; Scanlan 2009b; Poon-McBrayer and Wong 2013, Lane 2011; Sergeant and Berkner 2015; Lane, Kennison and Ellard 2019);

- Funding has been identified as the single largest barrier to the development of inclusive practice within Christian schools (Carlson 2014); and

- Efficacy of inclusive Christian education from the perspective of students, peers, families, teachers, and administrators is vital to understanding the development of an interdependent community (Pudlas 2004; Burke and Griffin 2010).

Prioritizing leadership, funding models, and program outcomes as areas for study will provide evidence needed for continuous program improvement and expansion of inclusive education in Christian schools.

Part II:
Perspectives on Inclusive Education

The Student Perspective
Elizabeth Lucas Dombrowski, *All Belong*

"*Nothing about us without us.*" This refrain of the disability rights movement underscores the importance of the voice of students with disabilities when educators plan, deliver, and evaluate programs and services. In keeping with this tenet of inclusive education, two alumni of an inclusive Christian school in Michigan participated in a focus group for this monograph.

Alex is a 2017 graduate who is a very social and outgoing adult, and he also has an intellectual disability. He loves music and seeing his friends as well as hanging out with his eight siblings. Abby, a 2012 graduate of the same inclusive Christian school, went on to earn a bachelor of arts in special education from Calvin University in 2016. She currently serves as an inclusive educator at another Christian high school in Michigan. The Christian high school attended by both of these alumni facilitated a robust social inclusion program called Connections, which involved hundreds of student volunteers with and without disabilities in activities like lunch buddies programs, after-school activities, an annual banquet, and peer tutoring.

Both Alex's and Abby's experiences suggest that when Christian school leaders and teachers take the time to truly listen to students with disabilities and involve them centrally in their own education, it can have a profound impact on their academic learning, personal and social development, and spiritual growth, as well as on the school community as a whole.

Q: *What did you appreciate the most about your high school experience?*

Alex: I had some really good friends that were part of Connections.

My favorite class was choir and shop. The teachers were the best. I had a solo in the final spring concert. I ran track, the 200 and the 400 meter races. It was really, really fun. The Connections banquet was the all-time high.

Abby: Even before high school, I'd always known that I wanted to be a teacher since I was in first grade. One day in middle school, I got really frustrated with one of my teachers for so often pairing me with students who were struggling. When I asked why, my teacher told me, "Well, Abby, you work really well with people who are different than you and you bring out the best in other people." And so that got my wheels turning. I've always loved everybody. Popularity was never something important to me. So I always just pulled in everybody.

I got involved right away in high school, starting off with Lunch Buddies [an inclusion program that pairs students with and without disabilities for lunch]. I think I spent more lunch hours with students receiving supports than I actually signed up for most weeks. It was just more fun in there! Lunches were an awkward time to begin with, and there was no cafeteria. And so, when you're standing in the hallway, like, OK, what do I do next? I don't want to go hide in the bathroom. So I just went to hang out with my buddies. And in my sophomore, junior, and senior years, I was part of the leadership team for Connections, which meant I helped plan all of the events and plan Lunch Buddies and schedule that.

Inclusion has always been part of my schooling experience. I can't imagine not having different learners in our classroom. It was just so much a part of everyday life. You see everybody in all of your classes. Being lab partners with a student receiving inclusion support when you were in science was no big deal because that's just how it goes. That was just so much a part of my high school experience that it was normal.

Q: *Can you imagine high school without that experience with Connections?*

Abby: No, I wouldn't have had any friends. In high school there can be drama between girls, and Connections was always the place that I knew I could go and be accepted and be loved no matter what. And I would love everybody in there, and people weren't mean to each other or petty, and there was none of the high school drama. The only drama was if you cheated at UNO. That was the only problem that happened in the room.

Alex: I was friends with Isaac. He is really cool guy. He was a really great friend. He's the best. And his mom works with special ed. We would have dinner and go to basketball games. And my friend Jacob went to Connections too. And we had fun at the banquet.

Q: *Alex, what was one of the most important things that you learned at school?*

Alex: Every day, I learned about the Lord, that he loves me and cares about me. Every, every day. And how to love other people, like your friends. And I love them—love all my friends—a lot.

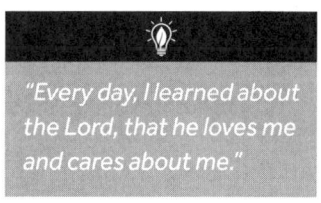

"Every day, I learned about the Lord, that he loves me and cares about me."

Q: *Abby, what did you as a student need—and what did other students need—in order to create a community of belonging, for students of all abilities?*

Abby: The biggest and most important thing was Mrs. Q [special education teacher]—just the support and the encouragement and just the way that she encouraged us all. She made us feel empowered to be able to do things on our own as high schoolers. This was important because high schoolers don't often feel empowered to do things. But she helped us feel empowered and she gave us leadership responsibilities. I think also the mutual support from everybody in Connections, knowing that was always a place to be safe and be loved. That was huge on both sides. It was always a judgment-free zone.

Q: *What are the benefits of inclusive education?*

Abby: Definitely richer education and richer friendships. And teachers learn to teach to a variety of abilities. You get things that you don't get from normal teaching when you're teaching to someone who struggles. Having people of all abilities made for an incredibly rich community where you felt loved and you felt like you belonged, no matter what your struggle was and no matter what your strengths were. You walk down the hallways and everybody knows everybody. Obviously it's high school, and so there's still the high school stuff that happens, but underlying it all is the love for everybody of all abilities.

> "Having people of all abilities made for an incredibly rich community where you felt loved and you felt like you belonged, no matter what your struggle was and no matter what your strengths were."

Alex: For students, if they didn't go to a Christian school, they might not know that what you learn is the Lord really loves me and cares about me.

Q: *Abby, how does inclusive education shape your career path, what you're doing now, and your faith?*

Abby: Inclusive education is just so built into who I am and what I do that it was no question to me. I graduated from Calvin and I knew exactly what I wanted to do. I wanted to do inclusive high school education. I wanted other high schoolers to have the kind of high school experience that I had, where you just have all of those different friends with different abilities. That was what I looked for when I was looking for a job. And that's where I am now—I'm doing high school inclusion and I'm doing my own version of the Connections program. We call it Sidekicks. I'm seeing friendships develop like the friendships that I had when I was in high school. Seeing just the smiles that come to my students' faces and my Sidekicks' faces. Some of the assignments that I give to my Sidekicks, listening to the reflections that they have, about what does it mean to have a friend with a disability? How has this changed how you are a friend to others, or how you even talk to your own friends about disabilities? That has been incredibly powerful to hear students' mindsets changing.

Q: *Why do you think inclusion is important for Christian schools? What would you want to tell leaders of Christian schools about inclusion?*

Alex: I tried to do my best every day, for my teachers. I would say students should go to see their principals and get to know them. I knew my principal and would go to see him every day. And principals should include all kids. Maybe support them as a group together, and they can be friends, and tell them that they're here to support them to have fun.

Abby: It's especially important for Christian schools because it truly reflects the body of Christ and the way that God has intended our world to be, with all people

> *"Inclusive education as a whole creates such a rich environment of learning."*

all together, all worshiping Him. Inclusive education as a whole creates such a rich environment of learning. In my job now, I have seen teachers totally change the way that they've been teaching for the last twenty years, because now they have different learners and they're like, wow, I didn't realize what I was doing doesn't actually work for kids. And so they have completely changed their philosophy of education. Inclusive education makes better teachers. It also makes better students. It makes students who are aware of others around them instead of just aware of themselves.

And inclusion just makes for a richer community. Having diversity in all aspects is so important, because it brings perspective and it brings meaning in ways that you don't have when you have all the same kind of people. That has just been such a solid foundation. And that has meant so much to me growing up and throughout my faith journey. The diversity of the body of Christ is one of my favorite things. Being people of all abilities, of all colors. And having that one solid base that connects us. I mean, there really are no words to describe how amazing that is!

The Parent Perspective
Matthew H. Lee, *ACSI*

A few days after she was born, our daughter was transported by medical helicopter to the children's hospital in Little Rock. Two weeks later in the NICU, she was diagnosed with a rare genetic disorder caused by missing segments of her fifteenth chromosome. She is, medically speaking, "missing a piece."

The combination of advancements in prenatal genetic screening and the ubiquity of abortion has led to a trend in wealthy countries of the disappearance (read: eradication) of certain congenital conditions. As long as the tragedy of legalized and normalized eugenics continues, it is possible that children with genetic disorders will become more common among Christians—who view all children as made in the image of God and gifts from him—than in the general population. This has been true in times past as well; since the Roman Empire, it has been the practice of faithful Christians to rescue the "weak" and "frail" children discarded by the pagan world (Craven 2010).

Congenital conditions are not the only reason for special education. But if the prevalence of children with disabilities among Christians rises relative to the general population, special education will increasingly become the exclusive concern of the Christian community.

What kind of education do I hope my daughter will receive? And why is my hope rooted in my faith?

Bearing the Image of God

Christians should deeply care about special education because all people bear the image of God. As Dutch theologian Herman Bavinck once wrote, "But among all creatures, only man is the image of God, the highest and richest revelation of God, and therefore head and crown of the entire creation" (qtd. in Hoekema 1986, 12; cf. Genesis 1:26-31). God continues to be intimately involved in the creation of each person who is formed, knitted together, and fearfully and wonderfully made by him, as Psalm 139:13-14 makes clear.

My wife and I take comfort in the knowledge that our daughter's condition is not the product of a random transcription error, but that she is known by God, precisely and purposefully created "that the works of God might be displayed" in her (John 9:3). We believe that her condition can only be explained as coming from God's hand, and since it comes from his hand, it can only be for our good (Ps. 119:71; Jer. 29:11) and for his glory (Ps. 118:23).

Christians who affirm the *Imago Dei* cannot but be deeply concerned for special education, for what reason could we justify the training up of some image bearers but not others? We learn from Genesis 1 that each image bearer is endowed with authority over all creation, created in fellowship with God and each other, and commanded to be responsible for filling the earth with God's glory. What do our special education practices teach our children and profess to an unbelieving world about our reliance on the sovereignty of God and the belief in the dignity of all people?

Children of the Covenant

We read in Acts 2 that Peter's sermon at Pentecost "cut to the heart" of those who were listening and left them wondering, "Brothers, what shall we do?" Peter replied, "Repent and be baptized every one of you in the name of Jesus Christ for the forgiveness of your sins, and you will receive the gift of the Holy Spirit. For the promise is for you and your children and for all who are far off, everyone whom the Lord our God calls to himself" (Acts 2:38-39). The inclusion of children in the blessings of the covenantal promise is an important reason for the practice of infant baptism in the Reformed tradition, of which my wife and I are a part (Westminster Confession of Faith, 28.4).

Regardless of their specific tradition, parents who choose a Christian education for their children often reference their desire to provide an education rooted in the faith. Christian educators emphasize the importance of schooling with a biblical worldview. We need to consider carefully what our special education practices teach our children—as well as profess to an unbelieving world—about the preeminence of our faith and confidence in the blessings of God's promises.

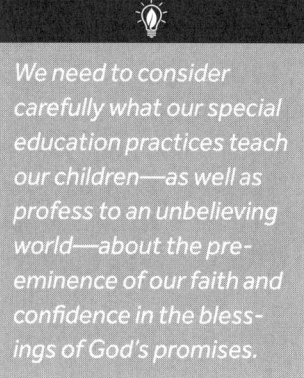

We need to consider carefully what our special education practices teach our children—as well as profess to an unbelieving world—about the preeminence of our faith and confidence in the blessings of God's promises.

The Missing Piece

I recently had the opportunity to speak with an inclusion specialist at a Christian school who shared this incredible story with me:

> I remember when the mother with a daughter with Down syndrome came in with a binder full of notes from all the schools she had been to. When she sat down with me, she said with tears in her eyes, "I really only have one question for you. If my child comes here, would you like my child?" I remember saying to her, "Would I like your child? I would love your child. Truly love your child. I believe that we are not whole without her here. Honestly, our school is missing something by not having her here. She is the missing piece."

For this educator, these were not mere high-minded, virtue-signaling moral platitudes geared towards persuading another tuition-paying parent to enroll her child in her school. Speaking of her special education students, she said, "These precious children help our students in greater ways than we support them and their families. They help our students look outside themselves. They start looking at the gifts that all students bring. They start to see the needs in others."

What a paradigm shift—to see students with disabilities not as people with challenges to be overcome, but as image bearers and heirs of the covenant promise (Heb. 6:17), and as such, the missing pieces we should earnestly desire for our schools.

> What a paradigm shift—to see students with disabilities not as people with challenges to be overcome, but as image bearers and heirs of the covenant promise (Heb. 6:17), and as such, the missing pieces we should earnestly desire for our schools.

God has already taught our family much. Our daughter's rare condition does not make her enigmatic, but precious (Gen. 41:38; Prov. 31:10). Her missing segments don't make her incomplete, but our family would be incomplete without her. She is and ever will be, as her middle name Dorothy suggests, a gift from God.

What about you and your school community? Could special education be the missing piece?

The Head of School Perspective
Interview with Rick Kempton, *Superintendent, Annapolis Area Christian School*

Rick Kempton has served as the superintendent of Annapolis Area Christian School (AACS) for the past nine years and has served on the ACSI Board of Trustees for 27 years, including two terms as board president. AACS is located in the metro DC area and enrolls 900 students in grades K-12 across four campuses. Prior to joining AACS, Rick worked in both Christian and public school education in Southern California. In this interview, ACSI's Director of Digital Initiatives, Sarah Loncar, asks Rick about his long-term commitment to inclusive education and AACS's ongoing journey toward serving students with disabilities with greater excellence.

Q: *How did your commitment to inclusive education develop?*

RK: When I think about the conviction that I have regarding why Christian schools should have an opportunity for kids that have different abilities, my conviction extends way beyond the years that I've spent here at AACS. It's really a part of who I am. And when I arrived here nine school years ago, that was a part of what I shared as my testimony when I was being interviewed. That's who I am. That's what I believe in. And I wanted to make sure that the people who were looking at me as a potential candidate knew that deep within me was a conviction about an opportunity for kids of all abilities to have a Christian education.

That conviction stems from a host of experiences. I was raised by a mom and a dad who both had childhoods filled with a lot of hardship. My mom was in twelve foster homes by the time she was in high school. My dad's father left his family when my dad was eight. And as a result, my mom and dad chose a life of service and care for others. I also have a younger brother who struggled with learning in the mainstream classroom. He had ADHD, but it surfaced during a time in education when we didn't know as much about it. As a result, he was underserved. And so I think those things contributed to the heart I have. And I began my career in public education, so I saw the services that were provided there. Then in 1984, I moved to a Christian school in Yorba Linda, California, where I served for 28 years. And I introduced meeting the needs of students with special needs into the program there right at the beginning. So that is part of the DNA that I brought to AACS.

Ultimately, I think inclusive Christian education is missional. I think it's biblical. I think everything about us as a Christian school screams at us to be inclusive. It gets me emotional when I think about the students that we lose at the admissions door, because they don't fit the mold of other families who may have children in our school. We make that decision sometimes because we don't know how to minister to the needs of that child. But we need to figure that out. It's for the individual student, yes, but the benefit is also cultural. I think one of the questions that we all have as heads of school is anytime we look at a new program or a new opportunity is, how will this impact our school culture? Inclusion makes a difference to the entire school. I watched the way our kids embrace those that maybe don't learn in the mainstream, may even look different—but the love is there and it makes a difference.

Q: *Can you share an example of culture-level change as a result of embracing students with disabilities?*

RK: I mentioned how inclusion was part of my heart, part of my conviction, before I even came on board at AACS. And once I was here, I was introduced to a dad here whose daughter, Jackie, has Down syndrome. Before I'd arrived, he'd been knocking on the door here for several years. He had his two sons in the school and he and his wife very much wanted Jackie to be a part of this. So we got acquainted. We went to lunch one day and began a conversation that has developed into a deep friendship. And as a result of that, we began talking and thinking about, how can we do this? How could we take the passion that he and I both have and convince those around us that this is something God is calling us to do? And he and I did that. He's been a tremendous resource financially to help us with this, but he's also been a driving force and an inspiration. I feel like together, God called us for such a time as this. With my arrival here, the denials he had received over the course of time, the passion he has for his family—those things came together and God used that to bring Jackie into our community.

She has been such an amazing addition. She has changed us because of who she is and it's been awesome to watch. And it's been so much fun to watch her move from our middle school to our upper school. And before long she'll graduate. She'll promote out of here. The experience has been valuable for her, but you know who has benefited most? It's us. It's our kids. One of the ways that's happened is that Jackie says hi to everyone, because she notices everyone. And that's had an effect on the school, in that because Jackie notices other students, it's helped students to notice other students. And when you are noticed by someone, it feels good. Then they go out and do the same thing because it just feels so good. They spread the love. We're in a "selfie" generation, but just seeing students notice each other just a little bit more, put down their phones, and think about someone else—that's huge. And that's just one of the things that happen here because Jackie was invited in to be a part of this. I think it changed hearts. It made a difference.

Part of what this experience has reinforced for us is that our school has a commitment to the whole family. I've seen this over and over again in my career, where child number one rolls through admissions and gets into our school. Then number two comes along, and now here's a child with disability that shows up at our admissions door, and now we say, "Nope, you can't come in here." That happens to families everywhere.

It's well known that Christian schools desire to partner with families. Should we only partner with part of the family? Should we only partner with the two that we say "fit," and then maybe there's one that doesn't? I don't think so, because I don't think that's the way God works. And so for us, and I know for other schools like us, they've embraced the whole family and said, "This is a ministry that we share a partnership between home and school, and we're loving all of you." And so we've made a decision that our commitment is to the family. When we embrace a family, we're embracing all of them and we must serve them to the best of our ability. We did that with Jackie's family and we're doing that with other families as well. It's a blessing.

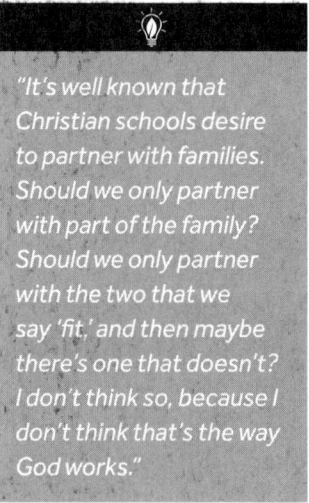

"It's well known that Christian schools desire to partner with families. Should we only partner with part of the family? Should we only partner with the two that we say 'fit,' and then maybe there's one that doesn't? I don't think so, because I don't think that's the way God works."

Q: What has been the most challenging part of the journey toward inclusion?

RK: When I think about the challenges of moving in the direction of inclusion in a Christian school environment, I've seen that it's difficult for people who aren't used to working with kids that might learn differently to understand that it's really something that God calls us to do. The fact is that God cares deeply about every child and all abilities.

In Christian schools sometimes we have expectations that might make it impossible for somebody with a disability to jump the hurdles we put in front of them. For example, if a school or an educator sees the main goal as college prep, they might think, *We can't maintain that standard if we have these kinds of kids.* I don't believe that either. I believe strongly that all God's kids get to be a part of this. All ability levels make for the best kind of campus culture. And that's what has helped me move through those periods of hesitancy and little speed bumps that people may have tossed in our direction.

The successes we have had have also moved us past those challenges— the lives of students that I see impacted, how it affects culture, and what it's done here at our school. Attitudes have changed—from some that didn't believe it could be possible, that now it's not only possible but also ideal, and a true blessing for all students and our whole school.

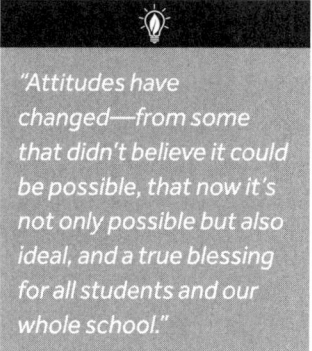

"Attitudes have changed—from some that didn't believe it could be possible, that now it's not only possible but also ideal, and a true blessing for all students and our whole school."

Q: *How did you help people transition from not thinking inclusion of students with disabilities is possible, to actually making it happen?*

RK: As I mentioned, this is my ninth school year here. And we have a strong culture of faculty and staff that love kids, care deeply about students, and develop relationships with them at every grade and every level. And yet working with kids that have specific kinds of disabilities and learning challenges was not something that was part of our culture. There was the hesitancy, this sense that "no, that's not us—we're not that kind of school." You need to get to a place of faculty buy-in, where you have overcome that initial hesitation.

I began looking for some resources, specifically that are available to us and to Christian schooling, that speak to this. I bumped into All Belong about five years ago. I got ahold of them, began talking to them, and I actually took a whole bunch of our folks to Grand Rapids, Michigan, to visit some of their partner schools. I selected our school principals to come along and I also picked people who I knew were influencers, who were also opposed to the idea of moving forward with this. I knew that if I convinced them that they would help influence others.

The visit was life-changing, because we saw how inclusion works. We saw evidence of it from K to 12 in all kinds of environments and all kinds of students with special needs and different kinds of situations and disabilities. I still remember when we came back to the airport and we huddled up to talk about it. We agreed right there that this was something we wanted to do. So I think the visit was significant in terms of showing us that, yes, we can do this and we have leaders who are ready to lead the way, from a place of deep hope instead of hesitancy or fear.

Since then, we've sent other faculty members a number of times so that they could actually see in practice what's happening in inclusive schools and what they're doing with kids who have disabilities. And we've partnered with All Belong in a consulting relationship. They have a representative who works with all four of our campuses, who is here three or four times a year for two or three days at a time. They have a very intuitive insight into who we are and it helps that we've had the same consultants since the beginning. All Belong has been a fantastic support to us because we've had somebody from the outside who can look in at us and help us see where we're making progress versus where do we need to take another look. They help us develop the policies that support what we're doing and help us to be consistent in doing the things that ultimately make a difference in the life of every child—not just splash a program on our website and say, "We have special education." And so I would say that the most instrumental piece of this has been the consulting relationship with All Belong.

I realize that every school has a different sized budget and a different capability to step into something that involves a consultant. If that isn't a possibility, there are other resources out there. At AACS we have people here, both staff and parents, who would welcome the opportunity to step into this with you. And so come talk to me, give me a call, write me an email, and I'd be happy to walk through this with other heads of school. However large or small your school is, there's a way to do this. 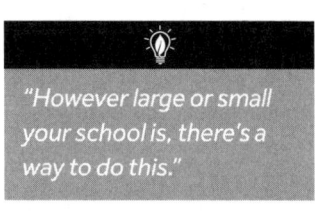 And it really begins with a willingness to step into the conversation, to ask the questions. How did you do it? How can we do it? How does this fit for

"However large or small your school is, there's a way to do this."

us? It starts with finding those who can sit down with you and look you in the eye and say, "Let me talk to you about the struggles that are still part of the journey, the things that make this hard, the victories that we look back on, the things we look ahead to that continue to drive us as something that we really believe God's called us to do."

Q: *Often school leaders view finances as a barrier to inclusion. Can you speak more to that specific barrier?*

RK: Every school is going to ask, "What's the financial feasibility of this and how do we sustain it?" For us, it's been a journey, in that we're continuing to look for ways to make this sustainable long-term and as feasible as possible. One of the things that's happened here is that God sent us somebody who is involved in a trust and believes in what we do, and they're contributing significantly. But the lion's share of what we invest still comes out of our school budget. We had to make a decision that we would, as best we could, fund this with tuition and gifts. There are some levels that we're still charging some families to receive services, but our goal would be to get to the place where we're not charging those folks any more money than regular tuition.

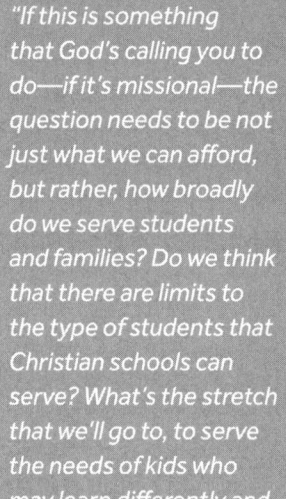

"If this is something that God's calling you to do—if it's missional—the question needs to be not just what we can afford, but rather, how broadly do we serve students and families? Do we think that there are limits to the type of students that Christian schools can serve? What's the stretch that we'll go to, to serve the needs of kids who may learn differently and have disabilities?"

It's acceptable in my mind to take a look at what your school is able to provide in terms of making sure that it's an excellent experience. And so for us, there are times and grade levels where we've identified we have "x" number of kids that are already receiving service and support at this grade level or maybe in this classroom. And as a result, we may have to say that for this year, it's not possible for us to enroll that additional child and to provide an excellent experience for them. But I would want it to be something that every school struggles with not just from a feasibility standpoint, but also from a missional standpoint. If this is something that God's calling you to do—if it's missional—the question needs to be not just what we can afford, but rather, how broadly do we serve students and families? Do we think that there are limits to the type of students that Christian schools can serve? What's the stretch that we'll go to, to serve the needs of kids who may learn differently and have disabilities? And I think that's a question that every school has to answer.

Q: *What parting advice would you give to heads of school who are thinking of deepening their commitment to inclusion?*

RK: I would say that I believe you can do far more than you think. For us, as we've developed this and grown our program, we've opened our door more widely than I think people thought we would at the beginning. And so we're learning about what that means and what that requires of us in terms of additional training for staff and faculty, and helping parents understand that this is what we're going to do to accomplish this.

Overall, I think the hesitancy to stop at that question of how do we afford it really, in my mind, can be overcome by asking the next question—"Is there someone who can help me do this?" I believe that there are heads of school like me, resources like All Belong, and folks in other schools that would say, "We can help you. We can help you figure this out if you believe this is what you should do." I hope people can look into my eyes and listen to me saying, "Yes, you can do this." And AACS would want to help. I want to be part of that support, and the community that we have here cares about that too. So, come join us.

Editor's Note: *For more information about AACS's journey, email Superintendent Rick Kempton at <u>rkempton@aacsonline.org</u>. All Belong resources can be accessed at <u>allbelong.org</u>.*

Part III:
Shaping Our Practice

The Inclusion Journey: From Program to Identity
Elizabeth Lucas Dombrowski, *All Belong*
Kate E. Strater, *Calvin University*

For many years, the answer to the challenges of disability in Christian education has been the formation of a *program*. It is easy to see how appealing this approach can be: programs give us neat boundaries and concrete edges, which in turn provide us with the confidence of knowing our capabilities and what our capacities are. Programs have understandably proliferated throughout our schools—from programs addressing dyslexia, to programs for students with autism, to programs for students with academic talents, to entire schools for students with a specific type of disability. In many cases, these programs do a world of good for students; they provide alternative teaching methods and create a space for students who otherwise would not have a place in the community.

But every teacher who has run one of these programs can think of a student who wasn't a good fit for that program. Perhaps it was a behavioral challenge, a communication problem, or lack of motivation. If the student leaves our community, our hearts might break for this outlier. Or, we may try to keep flexing the program to meet the student—for example, by creating a contract, which usually requires that the student change or perform in some way in order to remain in our programs. In response to such failures of fit, we often adjust the definition of who our schools are "meant" to serve; in other words, we might create admissions or tuition policies that define the level of academic or behavioral performance needed in order to enter our schools.

The underlying issue here is that programs by nature draw barriers—segregating students inside the program from those outside the program. These internal programs, then, begin to drive our definition of community, rather than the welcoming faith on which Christian schools are founded, as Jesus explains: "For I was hungry and you gave me food, I was thirsty and you gave me drink, I was a stranger and you welcomed me" (Matt. 25:35). What if—instead of waiting to see if a student can succeed within narrow parameters—we build schools that ensure students recognize the image of God in themselves and each other?

In this chapter, we propose that an identity-focused approach to inclusion—in which our schools' identities are as sites of inclusion—better proclaims our belonging to God, regardless of our own human limitations, in ways that a program-focused approach cannot. 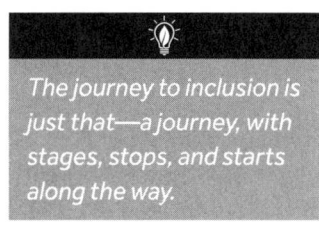 In recognition that the journey to inclusion is just that—a journey, with stages, stops, and starts along the way—we provide a series of reflective questions to help readers assess their school's progress from a program-centric approach, toward inclusion that operates on the level of school identity. This chapter is organized in four sections, to reflect four levels of our schools at which this journey toward inclusion occurs: 1) the learner; 2) the classroom; 3) the staff; and 4) the overall school culture (see Figure 1).

> The journey to inclusion is just that—a journey, with stages, stops, and starts along the way.

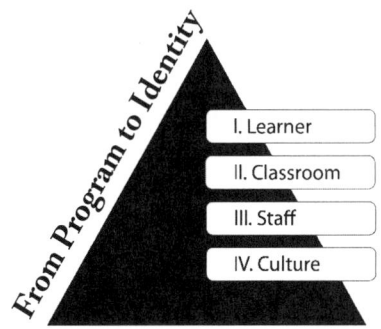

Figure 1. School Levels for the Inclusion Journey

Level 1: The Learner

How do we talk about the children who come to our school each day? Rather than semantics or an effort at political correctness, the language we use regarding students with disabilities in the Christian school is often reflective of what we *believe* about inclusion. Thus one of the first and most obvious clues to whether we are thinking in programs or in persons is the language we use.

What do we call our learners?

Each child, created in the image of God, is a unique blend of strength and ability paired with a variety of learning, social, physical, and spiritual needs. Person-first language reflects our belief that every student or individual is made in the image of God. Person-first language means that a person or their name is always referenced first, with their disability or diagnosis referenced secondarily (or not at all), so that we remind ourselves of our shared humanity first rather than our differences. It should be noted that uses of "typically abled" or "able-bodied" regarding students without disabilities are also not person-first language (All Belong 2018). Though this may change over time as kids grow, person-first language gives both students and educators a lens that emphasizes similarities, not differences.

Because we are discussing young people whose identities are still being shaped, we recommend using person-first language as a default. However, as students with disabilities grow and mature, they will typically develop a personal preference for how they would like to be described. Some may decide they prefer to be described with identity-first language, which respects the claimed identity of persons with

> *Because our language so often reflects the perspective we have of our students, we can purposefully harness our language to reflect God's love for them.*

disabilities—for example, "autistic" or "autistic person," or "deaf" or "blind." Such labels should only be applied after getting to know the individual with a disability and determining that, in fact, he or she prefers that terminology. Regardless of the specific words used or chosen, our guiding principle should be that because our language so often reflects the perspective we have of our students, we can purposefully to harness our language to reflect God's love for them.

How do we describe our learners?

In addition to person-centered language, school leaders need positive and thorough ways of describing students, their abilities, their strengths, and their limitations: "The better we know our learners, the more responsive we can be in our instruction. A learner profile describing a student's world and how that student makes sense of her world becomes a valuable decision-making tool" (Paxton-Buursma 2007, 10). There are many ways to describe students, but all should start with positive strengths and celebrate the gifts God has given to each one. Parents of students with disabilities, especially, are used to hearing overwhelmingly negative feedback about their children; instead, a Christian school on a journey toward inclusion can help students see their gifts and the unique roles they are called to play in community. This begins in the admissions process, which can be examined from a person-centered (versus program-centered) approach; in an inclusive school, the admissions process starts with the uniqueness of each student, as opposed to just a diagnosis or name of a disability. The underlying assumption is that the school context may need to change to fit the child—not the other

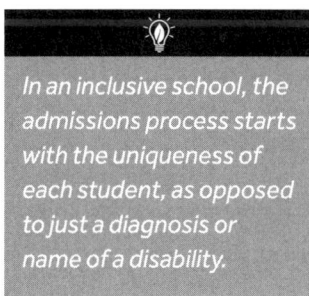

In an inclusive school, the admissions process starts with the uniqueness of each student, as opposed to just a diagnosis or name of a disability.

way around.

From admissions to the classroom and everything in between, our descriptions of learners should be "thick" or "rich," and can be gathered professionally with the help of school psychologists, or pieced together through learner observation, interviews, relationship development with students and families, and assessment. We grow our ability to plan and respond to the children we encounter by understanding what a child knows how to do; by exploring the child's cognitive, physical, social-emotional, and spiritual development; by understanding the child's culture; and by attending to the learning situation (Paxton-Buursma 2007). When it comes to difficult or challenging behavior, it is also helpful to remember the approach promoted by psychologist and author Dr. Ross Greene (2018): Behavior is communication. What are students trying to tell us through their behavior about their confidence, the academic or social skills they have yet to learn, or the trauma in their lives? It is much more effective to uncover the sources of disruptive behavior by getting to know the student and creating an environment that responds to their needs effectively. Planning can only be driven by a deep understanding and robust descriptions of the learner.

Level II: The Classroom

The context in which a child lives, learns, and plays has the potential to foster growth and community or marginalization and isolation. When the environment expects that a child should change to fit the context, the child's individual needs for community affirmation, feelings of social competence, and academic confidence often go unfulfilled. In a responsive context, the community responds in a manner that is supportive of the individual learner and honors learner diversity.

Responsive classrooms can go even further; they can foster

greater inclusion by anticipating that flexibility and change will be needed. They set aside time and space in advance to plan around the student needs that will arise. Responsive classrooms are in line with the biblical instruction to "warn those who are idle and disruptive, encourage the disheartened, help the weak, be patient with everyone" (1 Thess. 5:14, NIV). We can ask ourselves a number of questions to gauge where our schools are in the journey to responsive classrooms.

Do we use person-guided planning?

When students need an alternative course of study due to an intellectual or other disability, Person-guided planning can create a multidisciplinary curriculum that responds to individual student needs and growth. Allowing students and families to guide the process with their individual strengths and needs contrasts with a system-guided approach based in the status quo. Figure 2 defines the differences between beginning with the person or the system when creating individualized plans (All Belong 2020).

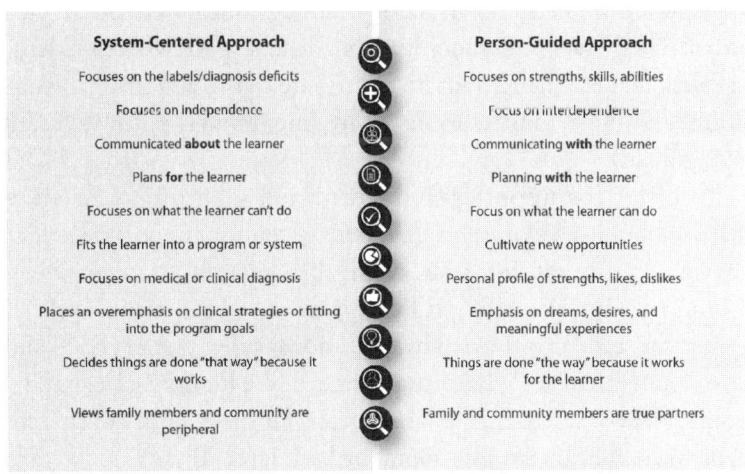

Figure 2. Person-Guided Planning Approach (from *All Belong—Person Guided Plan*)

The educational team serves as the ushers through this plan, thoughtfully asking about students' dreams and plans for the future. With those long-range dreams in mind, they are identifying the day-to-day supports that can help students achieve their individual dreams within the Christ-centered school's context. This includes building in opportunities to experience success at an appropriate level; after all, no student (or adult for that matter) enjoys spending the entire day doing the things with which they struggle!

By utilizing a thoughtful process that puts students at the center, school leaders create a space where students are celebrated for their ability to contribute to the educational community and opportunities to do so are intentionally cultivated.

The very nature of this approach pushes thinking beyond traditional systems related to standard classes and measurement of academic success. By utilizing a thoughtful process that puts students at the center, school leaders create a space where students are celebrated for their ability to contribute to the educational community and opportunities to do so are intentionally cultivated (All Belong 2020).

In order to support person-centered planning, Christian schools should develop a multi-tiered system of supports. Educators may be most familiar with this system in terms of a response-to-intervention (RTI) approach, which tiers levels of support for students provided by educational support staff (ESS) and classroom teachers by level of student need (see Figure 3). In a multi-tiered system of supports, the school plans for the majority of student needs to be met in the classroom, or base level. There is a possible transition to the next level of the pyramid, where interventions are provided based on screening tools and data measurement. Students in this second level are expected to move fluidly back and forth between the first and second level. If data measurement continues to show a lack of progress for a student, they might be provided more significant supports or a modified curriculum at the top, or third, level of the pyramid.

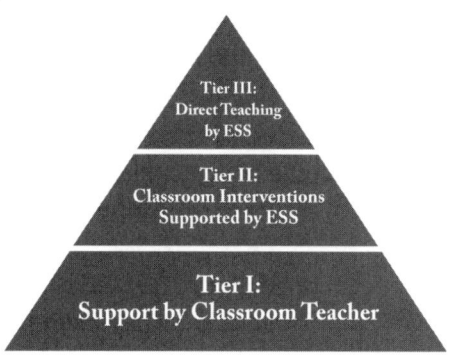

Figure 3. Christian School Multi-Tiered System of Supports

Do we provide responsive behavior support?

Person-guided planning also provides a path for a positive and supportive educator response to student behavior. As mentioned earlier, challenging behaviors are not usually what they seem at first glance. Developing descriptively thick learner profiles provides insight into behavior and surrounding contexts, growing the educator's ability to respond to a child's behavior with positive and productive support. This is particularly important in determining where behaviors are resulting from a mismatch between classroom structures and individual weaknesses in developmental areas (Barringer, Pohlman and Robinson 2010), which Greene (2018) describes in terms of lagging academic or social skills.

The classroom can be structured to ensure individual supports for students in five key ways: 1) identifying and responding to sensory and physical needs; 2) making sure students are engaging in positive, meaningful experiences; 3) implementing scaffolds, structure, and support; 4) removing barriers to full participation; and 5) identifying skills to that students need to be taught (Aspy and Grossman 2008). Collaboration in providing these supports—between peers, teachers, administrators, and support staff—creates opportunities for proactive, comprehensive social-emotional learning activity within the school day. Collaboration has the added benefit of "simultaneously teach[ing] some very important skills: empathy, appreciating how one's actions are affecting others, resolving disagreements without conflict, taking another person's perspective, and honesty" (Greene 2018, 26).

Do we facilitate peer support for students with disabilities?

Peer support is a collaborative strategy that places children together in pairs or small groups to learn and grow academically, socially, and spiritually. Research has shown positive results related to student achievement and a sense of belonging, enhancing instruction and relationship development for all students (Riester-Wood 2015). Peer relationships can have an effective and valid impact on learning for all students; we have even seen some cases where they have reduced the need for paraeducators or one-on-one aides.

The benefits of authentic friendship for students with significant disabilities cannot be understated, but often have just as many benefits for students who simply struggle to succeed in academics. As one parent of a student who struggled through high school shared about inclusive education efforts, "You gather up not only inclusion students in our schools, but all those students who may be wandering through their education" (Dombrowski 2017).

Do we engage students in social emotional learning?

Social emotional learning holds much promise for empathy development, relationship-building, and collaborative problem-solving in the classroom. While there are many different approaches that we could highlight, one example of social emotional learning that is gaining traction in the Christian school context is restorative practice. Although not developed from faith-specific communities, restorative practice paints a picture of *shalom*—that holy peace and recognition of God's image in each other. Such practices free up our schools to focus on the life-giving Gospel that we are called to share, rather than on the restrictions of program boundaries that primarily spotlight the fallen nature of our world.

Examples of these kinds of practices range from being intentional with affective language to pre-scripted circles and conferences. Affective statements frame teachers' feedback to each other and our students in a positive light, by using "I" statements and expressing feelings in private (versus in front of the entire class). For example, instead of saying "stop that," we would pull a student aside privately and instead say, "I worry about other kids' safety when you push them in the halls." Restorative questions focus on retelling the story of a conflict, using key guided questions to find resolution. Restorative circles can be used proactively to build community and responsibility when harm has occurred.

In each of these examples, the teacher is in the role of asking good questions, as well as listening openly and humbly to the answers. Children have an opportunity to speak and listen to each other in a safe environment, opening the door to multiple perspectives and the development of stronger relationships and positive behaviors (Schott Foundation et al. 2014). Through this practice of empathy, school leaders honor student voice and help students find resolutions that bring everyone back into community (rather than exclusionary punishment), thereby modeling even more distinctly the *shalom* that God desires for Christian communities.

Level II: The Staff

Responsive contexts are sustained through inclusive and responsive practices and policies. But perhaps most importantly, they are designed, implemented, and embodied by school staff. School communities built upon inclusive leadership and collaboration among staff have a strong foundation from which to respond to diverse learners.

Does school leadership truly lead in the area of inclusion?

There are many facets of leading an inclusive Christian school; here we focus on the practices and policies that leaders may enforce or create. The school leader is uniquely positioned to hold the school staff accountable to their collective commitments; this may mean asking for data, following up on the delivery of supports, and holding the school accountable to research-based teaching practices.

Barringer, Pohlman, and Robinson (2010) describe leaders' engagement in fostering inclusion in terms of understanding variation in learners; gathering evidence to understand how specific students learn; engaging in a problem-solving process to discover and encourage learner strengths, while supporting learner weaknesses; identifying core beliefs about how all learners will be treated within the school; and development of school policy and practice aligned with support for varying learners. The leader's role in each of these is visioning, fostering, and modeling of skills; cultivating inclusive leaders within the community; and inviting students into this community—built upon the recognition of all members as image bearers of God.

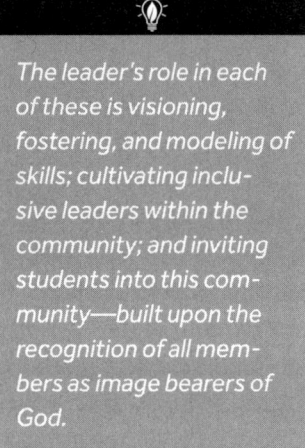

The leader's role in each of these is visioning, fostering, and modeling of skills; cultivating inclusive leaders within the community; and inviting students into this community—built upon the recognition of all members as image bearers of God.

How well do our teachers collaborate with educational support staff?

When building an inclusive Christian school, the role of educational support services is key to a successful culture. Whether or not these roles fall on full- or part-time staff, they are responsible for advocating for students' needs and supporting their success in community. The overarching goal of all educational support services is toward inclusion and the building of a Christ-centered community where all students have a chance to use and grow their gifts.

Even with an articulated vision in place, staffing can pose a major hurdle for Christian schools on the journey toward inclusion. Public school-focused training often does not prepare staff for the context of Christian education, even though as Lane (2017) points out, special education staff with such training are often tasked with creating the programs, policies, and procedures needed for student success. On the flip side of the coin, many teachers—more than half in one study—serving in these roles in Christian schools have no training in the field of special education whatsoever (Lane 2017).

Christian schools puzzling over how to staff for inclusion may find a way to move forward by focusing on roles instead of specific job titles or positions. Focusing on fulfilling roles can allow for flexibility in staffing arrangements, while ensuring that students' needs will be effectively met. All Belong has identified five roles that such staff members must fill to create a culture of inclusion: 1) consultative; 2) diagnostic; 3) teaching; 4) supervisory; and 5) advocacy, as follows.

- The *consultative role* is perhaps the most visible role that support staff fill in the school and requires significant collaboration with general education teachers on behalf of students who may be at risk in the general learning environment. This could include brainstorming or observing on issues of academic adjustment, social development, behavioral changes, or on strategies of universal design. They meet regularly with colleagues as part of an overall multi-tiered system of supports, ensuring adequate progress is made by all students and targeting supports to those who may need it.

- The *diagnostic role* may often require more specialized training in order to evaluate student progress on an individual basis. In this role, support services teachers are digging to find out more about the students in their school and may use a variety of testing systems in order to do so. It is important to validate any tests being used in order to ensure that identification of areas of struggle recognize the diversity of student experience. In Christian schools, fulfillment of this role may often be sought outside of the school, but it is important for staff to engage diagnostic results showing a pattern of strengths and weaknesses while maintaining a Christ-centered, biblically based view of each student as uniquely made in God's image.

- The *teaching or remediation role* of support services is the most segregated aspect of an inclusive Christian school, but students with significant needs often require some one-on-one teaching. These roles may occur in a variety of settings, whether push-in, pull-out, and many options in between. However, the key for inclusive schools is to not prioritize this aspect of the role at the expense of all others, with the result that direct teaching comes to be seen as the primary solution for struggles in the general education classroom. This is not only untrue but also creates a self-fulfilling process that can ultimately undermine inclusion (i.e., as the support services teacher provides more and more direct teaching, they have less time for consultation with general education teachers; then without adequate support, general education teachers identify a need for more pull-outs, which reinforces the view that direct teaching services are the only remaining way to meet students' needs).

- This points to the importance of the *supervision role*. When it comes to paraeducators, expectations must be set from an inclusive standpoint, with oversight and appropriate training provided by the school, so they can act as a bridge—not a barrier—for students' success in community.
- Finally, the *advocacy role* involves support services staff members providing advocacy on behalf of students in an inclusive school. This positions them in the role of partner—not adversary—to parents of students with disabilities. Through this role, support staff can beautifully embody the Christian school's commitment to partnering with parents as they seek to fulfill their God-given (Deuteronomy 6) responsibilities of training up their children.

Level IV: School Culture

When operating from a faithful and faith-filled welcoming perspective of each student, Christian schools have many assets that allow for serving students with disabilities—especially as they move toward inclusion at the level of the learner, the classroom, and the staff. The practices outlined in these preceding three levels become deeply intertwined, especially as inclusive education efforts evolve from a program to a system approach. As that system evolves and reinforces belonging for all students, it grows into an identity approach—first for the Christian school's identity, as inherently and especially inclusive; and concurrently as a personal identity for all students as learners in a context that centers their unique gifts and strengths. In other words, when taken together, inclusion at these levels becomes more than the sum of its parts. And it is at this level of culture that the transformation from program to school identity becomes fully possible.

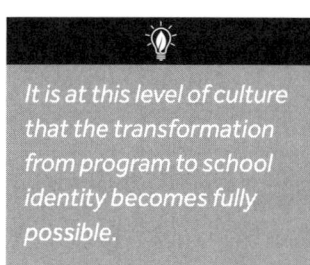

It is at this level of culture that the transformation from program to school identity becomes fully possible.

A key component of culture-level change is cross-constituent collaboration, with teachers, administrators, families, and the wider community to meet the needs of students. This might mean inviting volunteers or donors into the dream for inclusive education. It might mean scheduling aside time for collaborative meetings to review student progress, and it certainly means clear and helpful communication about a student's goals to all those involved in the student's education. Yet within that flexibility and openness, students deserve the best of what we know can be effective for their education. This requires a rigor of accountability, ensuring that every intervention is accomplishing what we expect it to. And when the old tried-and-true strategies fail, we must be willing to get creative to meet the educational goals for each student.

The journey toward inclusion in the Christian school—from programs that serve students with disabilities, to a school identity that reflects an inclusive culture—is certainly not an easy one. But as other authors from various roles and backgrounds attest in this monograph, this journey is entirely worthwhile—both for students who are uniquely created in the image of God, and for Christian schools seeking to reflect God's extravagant love to the families and broader communities they serve.

Reimagining Finance and Sustainability: From Limits to Possibilities
Elizabeth Lucas Dombrowski, *All Belong*
Matthew H. Lee, *ACSI*

As leaders of nonprofit organizations, we are often called to do what seems impossible: provide high-quality Christian education at the lowest possible price. This demand could come from our board, the community, or the realities that any given year's budget might present. But the pressure is always there to set budget numbers that work, to hit our goals, and ultimately to sustain our organizations responsibly.

Providing the educational supports to meet the needs of every student, however, should not be simply a question of budget. It is possible and entirely within reason for every Christian school to set aside the question of whether a student's needs can be met with current resources, and to instead ask, *what would it look like if their needs were met here?* It is a subtle but powerful difference in posture: one gives power to *limits*, the other gives power to *possibilities*. We must give ourselves permission to dream, and to do so with the involvement of our community.

Not only is the inclusion journey possible, but it is also a proven one in many Christian schools—even if it often has humble beginnings. One Christian school inclusion specialist we spoke with recalled a time when special education at her school was nothing more than a resource room: "One summer I was approached by the principal and asked to work as an inclusion aide for a student with a visual impairment. I thought, 'I don't know anything about students with visual impairments.'" Had she focused on the limits of her abilities, or had her school focused the limits of its resource room, this student may have been denied the opportunity to enroll. Instead, she reimagined the possibilities—focusing on small but meaningful steps, like taking online Braille classes to better support the student.

Giving power to possibilities transformed the special education culture of her school. "Over time," she continued, "our board decided that we had people in our system who were able to fulfill those responsibilities. We started hiring our own inclusion coordinators. We started hiring our own special educators." As the school prioritized the mission of serving families and reimagined the budget around possibilities rather than limits, they came to develop one of the most highly regarded special education programs in the state—public or private.

Every Christian school can budget and support a robust and inclusive program that is more representative of kingdom diversity. In this chapter, we hope you will find some insights into reimagining special education finance. We begin by explaining how our budgets communicate our covenantal values and our commitment to building inclusive communities. Next, we describe the relationship between inclusion and sustainability in Christian schools, followed by identification of school budgeting and management practices to this end. We conclude with an encouraging story regarding growing our faith in God's ability to provide as we move from limits to possibilities.

Communicating Our Values

Budgets can be great tools for planning, but they are also tools for communication. They communicate our mission, our priorities, and our faith in God to provide for our needs (Gen. 22:14). Yet, a budget can also be used as a shield—to give us the power of saying no, and in doing so, to draw the line between limits and possibilities. We must never lose sight of the fact that a budget reflects the values of the school. What does your budget say about your school's values when it comes to students with disabilities?

Principles must provide the foundation for practices. If a school affirms that children with disabilities bear the image of God and have claim to the blessings of covenantal promises, it must find a way to align its practices with its principles. Committing to these principles takes more than love for all of God's children; it takes disciplined budget-setting practices. As the apostle Paul explains in 2 Timothy 1:7 (NIV), "For the Spirit God gave us does not make us timid, but gives us power, love and self-discipline." Schools must apply these Spirit-led qualities in setting an annual budget. Many schools have been given the resources to demonstrate love and self-discipline in setting budget goals that reflect their faith, not their timidity.

Applying power, self-discipline, and love to a school budget may seem intimidating, but as former Liberian President Ellen Johnson Sirleaf once said, "If your dreams do not scare you, they are not big enough" (Sirleaf 2011). Perhaps in the Christian school context, dreams that do not scare us are not faithful enough. Our self-discipline must come together with our faith to demonstrate God's power over and over again, in order for Christian schools to fulfill their promise to be healthy, vibrant, and biblically based communities.

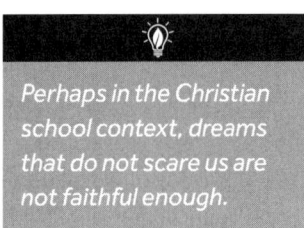

Perhaps in the Christian school context, dreams that do not scare us are not faithful enough.

Inclusive Education and Sustainability

Many schools approach the path of inclusion with an eye toward sustainability. And thankfully, when we are called to a clear mission, God is with us in it. We do not take this challenge of funding for inclusive education lightly, but seek to challenge the traditional assumptions that often underlie and limit a budget-based conversation about meeting the needs of all students.

Imagine a parent of four school-age children contacted your school for enrollment. Just as 14 percent of the U.S. school-age population has a disability (Hussar et al. 2020, 40), one of their children has autism spectrum disorder (ASD). It is still too early to tell how much this will impact their child's learning, but these parents want assurance that your school will commit to the journey of Christian education with them for the next decade, if not longer. If you make this commitment, including to the child who may have more significant needs, all of the family's students will come and pay full tuition. Since fewer and fewer parents wish to travel to more than one school every morning, this family represents an all-or-nothing proposition for your school: if you cannot enroll the student with ASD, you will not enroll any of the students in this family.

This scenario is not uncommon, and it exemplifies the budgetary ties between meeting the needs of students with disabilities and enrollment growth. Inviting students with disabilities into our schools can be a recruitment and retention strategy, not just for families with significant disabilities but potentially many more families. Inviting students with disabilities means inviting families into our schools, which in turn provides access to larger groups of families for recruitment. When parents enroll their students as preschoolers or kindergarteners, they typically have no way of knowing the challenges their student might face (e.g., struggling to read, confusion in math, missing social cues, or even a concussion in middle school). Seeing that their child's school is committed to students at every level of ability can increase parent confidence that the school is just as committed to their child as it is to others.

Interestingly, the coronavirus pandemic proved in concept that offering special education services can be a financially sustainable strategy for Christian schools. A COVID-19 research report from the Association of Christian Schools International found that "the combination of opening on campus and increasing support for special education (SPED) students was particularly meaningful." Specifically, enrollment levels at schools that did both were *9.9 percent higher than before the pandemic*, while levels at schools that "reopened with blended or distance-only instruction and decreased SPED support *declined by over 20 percent*" (Swaner and Lee 2020, 9, emphases added).

Finally, it is helpful to view the relationship between inclusion and Christian school sustainability against larger economic trends in the educational sector. One such trend is the reality that more and more families are turning to private schools—not public schools—to access the best education and services for their children. It shouldn't come as a surprise that families are increasingly turning to private schools to meet their unique educational needs. According to Claypool and McLaughlin (2017), as the incidence of conditions like ASD increases and the standard of care for children with disabilities improves, "families look to the private sector, not public schools" for the best educational experience for their children. The authors continue:

> Parents want control of the special education dollars to obtain the best services possible whether in public schools, private schools or behavioral clinics. This is fuel for greater educational choice, which expands families' access to more high-quality schools and services that fit their needs.

Unsurprisingly, public opinion polls reveal that most people favor providing education savings accounts or vouchers to families of students with higher needs (DiPerna, Catt and Shaw 2020). Christian schools can investigate and support school choice funding in their states as they seek to offer special education services and support meaningful educational progress for a more inclusive student population.

Research on private schools and special education finds they are capable of enrolling students who need more significant services (Greene 2007; Greene and Winters 2007), delivering higher levels of satisfaction (Greene and Forster 2003; Weidner and Herrington 2006; Varga et al. 2021), and operating special education without breaking their budgets (Greene and Buck 2010). What is needed is a mindset change about special education in Christian schools: Christian schools can afford to offer special education services and support meaningful educational progress for a more inclusive student population.

School Budgeting and Management Practices

Some practices help build inclusive communities at the expense of balanced budgets. Others are fiscally sound but are not conducive to full inclusion that prioritizes a sense of belonging for all students. In this section, we identify four practices that are both inclusive and sustainable: tuition equity; "whole-family" policy; multi-tiered system of supports; and fundraising.

Tuition Equity

Sustainably pursuing inclusive education does not automatically equate to charging parents of students with disabilities significantly more than other students. Tuition equity—the practice of charging all students the same in tuition regardless of their level of ability—is achievable for all Christian schools and it sends a powerful message of Christ's love and openness to all students.

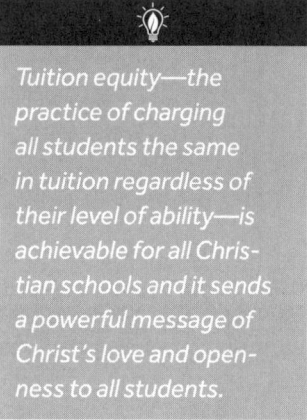

Tuition equity—the practice of charging all students the same in tuition regardless of their level of ability—is achievable for all Christian schools and it sends a powerful message of Christ's love and openness to all students.

When some schools adopt tuition equity as a policy, tuition rates might increase slightly more than usual. This was certainly the case in the early 1990s, when several partners of All Belong (the Christian Learning Center at the time) adopted this policy, including the aforementioned inclusion specialist's school. To ensure that supports could be provided for all students, all parents accepted an initial tuition increase—following good and proactive communication by school leadership around the philosophical and theological reasons for the increase, as a reflection of the community that the school was trying to build.

By anticipating and expecting the diversity of humanity, tuition equity even becomes countercultural in its inclusiveness. As Hoeksema (2007) states:

> A subtle but insidious implication of talking about including students who are frequently excluded in schools is that it can perpetuate a kind of "us-them" thinking. There are those who need special treatment in order to be successfully integrated into typical school environments, and then there's the rest of us. The truth is, "they" are not to be included or excluded by "us." They are us. No more expendable. No less esteemed. No more a burden. No less a gift. (3)

Charging more in tuition for the subset of the student population who may need support (as opposed to, for example, not charging extra for participation in sports teams, the arts, honor societies, or other "talent"-based offerings) is a powerful separation technique, one that assumes students who need additional support are somehow less worthy of school and donor investments. Where that assumption may be present in our schools, it is time to examine it critically and invite the school community into an alternative vision of gospel living.

Along these lines, inclusive education plays an important role in Christian schools achieving their mission for all students. A national study of over 15,000 Christian school constituents found that *all* alumni of Christian schools that meet the needs of students with disabilities are 1.8 times more likely to report that they are walking with God (Swaner, Marshall and Tesar 2019). This suggests that caring well for students with disabilities within a school community can have a lasting impact on the faith development of all students. This is consistent with other studies on the whole-school impact of inclusion, which "has produced a generation of general education students who have become much more open-minded and willing to receive the gifts offered by people who too often are characterized by their perceived inabilities or needs" (Van Dyk 2010, 383).

In one All Belong video about the inclusion of one student named Isaac, the administrator shared that, "When we do inclusion, we find that whole classes become more understanding of each other." And the special education teacher reflected, "I think the blessing of having Isaac here at school really has been about seeing God at work in a very real way, every day" (All Belong 2018). If inclusion benefits all students within a given school community—as research suggests—then tuition equity is truly an equitable approach.[1]

A "Whole-Family" Policy

There's another side to the tuition equity coin, however. A covenantal bond between a school and its families means that on the one hand, a school won't charge a family more for some of their children than others. But on the other hand, it means that families can show good faith by enrolling all of their children. In practice, many schools implement a "whole-family" policy alongside a tuition equity policy.

In such a policy, families are asked to commit to partnership with

---

[1] A caveat: when discussing tuition equity, tutoring services are not the same as inclusive education systems and supports. While they may be an important tool for some students, by nature when tutoring services are optional, those should not be considered part of a multi-tiered system of supports. Tutoring services respond to parental choice and optional buy-in, while the essential education of students based on their needs is provided as part of the school's core educational product.

the school and practice their faith by sending all eligible children to the same Christian school. If the family elects to send only their students with significant needs for support, and other eligible students are in the public school, that family may be charged more in tuition. There are many ways this is lived out, and there are often exceptions for various reasons, but the goal is for the family and the school to be long-term partners in education.

Multi-Tiered System of Supports

A multi-tiered system of supports can help a school manage the extra costs associated with operating a special education program (this system of supports was described earlier in Chapter 7). With tuition equity, all levels of intervention can be provided based on an individual student's level of need, not on parents' ability to pay or advocate. The model of equity recognizes the complexity of student learning, and that students may be moving around and between these levels throughout their school career. By implementing a holistic approach to special education, the school frees itself to provide the supports that a student may need at any given moment, and to change the level of support provided when it is no longer in the students' best interest. It also avoids dichotomizing a school's student population into "general education" and "special education" students, thereby building a more inclusive school community.

Fundraising

Fundraising is not just a method of making the budget work while providing supports for students. It is an opportunity to invite the community into the mission of the school and, ultimately, of being part of the body of Christ. For theologians like Henri Nouwen, it is an opportunity to help the donor discover God's calling on their life: "Fundraising is a very concrete way to help the kingdom of God come about" (2010, 24). Schools gain incredible strength and power in this effort when fundraising is combined with inclusion. When schools fundraise for inclusion, they cast a vision of belonging for every student—ensuring that students' needs are met and that achievement is not a prerequisite for belonging in a Christ-centered community. Fundraising thus creates an opportunity for the school community to rally around students with more significant needs.

Prospective donors are often moved to generosity by opportunities to support students with disabilities. From a practical side of things, the next time you talk with a successful entrepreneur in your community, find out how school went for them. Did they struggle? Did they ever feel like they weren't the smartest kid? If you share your goal and your vision of being a place of belonging for every student, especially those that remind them of themselves, you may open up an entirely new funding source.

On a cautionary note regarding fundraising for inclusion, it is again important to be cognizant of the ways in which our images and words reinforce a sense of division between "us" and "them." Support services benefit all students through the model of interventions and support, so case-for-support pictures might not always show students with visible disabilities. To honor the *Imago Dei* of students with disabilities—something with which our surrounding culture continually struggles—we should avoid pity-based messages or pictures, and instead do all we can to represent visually and verbally the interdependent community we are trying to build for students of diverse abilities (Barkley 2019).

> When schools fundraise for inclusion, they cast a vision of belonging for every student—ensuring that students' needs are met and that achievement is not a prerequisite for belonging in a Christ-centered community.

Growing Our Faith

In conclusion, much as we need stories to guide us in Christian faith, we need stories to guide us through inclusion. There will be twists and turns, confusing situations, and mistakes. As Danforth (2014) encourages, "Successful inclusive educators do not ignore the gap between their ethical beliefs and their daily work in schools. They intentionally toil in the gap" (18). It helps to know that others are often struggling with the same challenges you may face, especially when attempting to align policies with beliefs.

One of my (Elizabeth's) favorite stories at All Belong is that of a student with significant learning and medical needs who applied to a Christian school known for inclusion. This situation was a stretch for the school financially, and they thought they had supports and services lined up to be provided by the state. Three days before school started, the state backed out of their offer. Over the weekend, the deacons of the student's local church prayed and considered whether they could provide the funding to the school. They could not, and I called the school the next morning with a heavy heart. To my delight, however, a donor had just come through with a gift that covered funding for the student's entire first year.

But this isn't the best part of the story. By October, the student's classmates had started a campaign to raise money for the next year, to ensure she could come back. This is a community embracing inclusion and the role that every person can play in building the body of Christ. This is building a budget that reflects our values and allowing room in that budget for God to work a few miracles along the way. This is the power and love that the Spirit gives us, to build our school communities in, through, and for Christ. This is moving from limits to possibilities.

Recommended Resources

We conclude this monograph with a selection of helpful resources and references that are intended to inspire and support the journey toward inclusion in Christian schools. The resources listed below follow this page, in order:

1. **The Christ-Centered Support Services Standard overview.** ACSI REACH Accreditation makes the All Belong protocol available to interested schools as an endorsement.

2. **Continuum of Attitudes Toward People with Disabilities in Christian Schools.** Developed by Ability Revolution and reprinted with permission, this resource depicts a continuum of student views and beliefs about inclusion in the Christian school.

3. **Getting Started with the Team in an Inclusive Setting guide.** This resource helps to answer the question, "You have enrolled a student in need of an individualized curriculum and a part-time paraprofessional—now what?"

4. **All Belong Person-Guided Transition Planning excerpt.** This excerpt of a larger guide to inclusion in Christian schools shares information on philosophical foundations for inclusion, belonging planning for students, the student's circle of support, the facilitator's role, and discussion topics for middle and high school transition planning.

5. **Recommended Books for Further Reading.** A list of books for further reading, developed by the monograph's authors, is cited.

All resources from All Belong are reprinted with permission; visit allbelong.org to explore their catalog of resources, which is continually updated. The Wheaton Center for Faith and Disability also offers a number of resources, which can be accessed at https://www.wheaton.edu/wheaton-center-for-faith-and-disability/.

ACSI Leading Insights

V. The Indicators

Standard: A Christ-centered school which fully includes children and young people of all abilities creates a culture that equips each pupil to actively contribute in the life of the school community.

Each Indicator of this Standard is organized into a Category.

COMMUNITY
All stakeholders demonstrate an intentional and comprehensive commitment to all learners.

1.1 A mission for including and welcoming students is expressed clearly in writing and in person by and to all stakeholders, and reflects a Biblically-based view of the child.

1.2 Admissions and enrollment policies seek to enroll whole families, welcoming students with a high level of support needs as well as those with mild accommodations.

1.3 General education teachers show a sense of ownership toward students with identified disabilities, fostering a welcoming environment with age-appropriate peers and a desire to support every learner.

1.4 Educational services staffing is adequate and appropriate to the size and needs of the school's student body.

1.5 The school understands and honors each student as a member of the body of Christ, using descriptive common language and flexible services.

1.6 Educational services are provided for every student in a way that is financially equitable.

COLLABORATION
School staff functions in a collaborative manner to educate the whole student.

2.1 Staff use effective communication strategies within a defined process for collaboration and communication on behalf of individual students.

2.2 Personalized student goals are developed and shared collaboratively among teachers, administrators, parents, and the student themselves.

2.3 Personalized student support plans address the whole child, including his/her relationships with God and with peers.

2.4 A process is in place and followed that provides evidence of progress on personalized student plans.

2.5 All staff receive ongoing professional development with purposeful follow-up that equips them to teach students with varied abilities.

2.6 School staff and parents are aware of what is available and provided to the students both internally and by outside contractors, whether through public school districts or private partnerships.

CULTURE
The school community has developed a culture of belonging.

3.1 Students with and without disabilities develop socially and emotionally together with their age-appropriate peers.

3.2 The school's physical spaces and usage plans have been designed to take into account accessibility, convenience, and social inclusion of persons with disabilities.

3.3 Individuals within the school readily and whole-heartedly celebrate diversity of abilities in their communities.

3.4 The community engages in processes of recursive self-assessment to educate all students most effectively.

all belong

Shaping Our Practice

CONTINUUM OF ATTITUDES TOWARDS PEOPLE WITH DISABILITIES IN CHRISTIAN SCHOOLS

Uninformed Observer	Sympathetic Bystander	Active Helper	Compassionate Peer	Reciprocal Friendship
"Some of the students at the Christian school where I attend have problems reading and paying attention. The teachers end up spending more time with them during class, but what they really need is extra tutoring. I'm assuming they were admitted because they are good at sports. I don't have anything against them, but I think they need to be held to the same academic standards as everyone else."	"Some of the kids at my school volunteer to work with handicapped kids at annual summer respite retreats. I feel sorry for the families who have kids with physical and health issues. It must be tough to be in a wheelchair and to be so different from everyone else. I can't imagine not being able to walk or to see or to hear. I'm so glad that God has blessed my family and me with the gift of healthy physical bodies."	"My friends and I volunteer to help kids with disabilities by having a charity basketball event each year. We invite kids with special needs from other schools. We have a club that helps raise awareness to eliminate the R-word, and to raise money for people with disabilities. A few of us volunteered to serve food at church prom event for people with disabilities. It's cool to be able to spend time with people who need our help."	"We have a separate classroom at our Christian school for students with disabilities. They attend chapel with us and we include them in some of our social clubs and after-school activities. I serve as a peer mentor, and it's great having them on our school campus. Our student body leadership team nominated a kid named Mike who has autism as Homecoming King so that he would feel special."	"Joe is one of my best friends and he is really good at math. He's honest and he tells it like it is. I helped him practice asking a girl to the prom because sometimes he's not so good with his social skills. My other friend David makes me laugh with his funny jokes. Sometimes he asks me for help with counting change when we eat lunch in the cafeteria together. I couldn't imagine not having Joe and David at my school."

2/2/18

http://AbilityRevolution.org

99

CENTER FOR INCLUSIVE EDUCATION

Getting Started with the Team
in an Inclusive Setting

You have enrolled a student in need of an individualized curriculum and a part-time paraprofessional. Now what?

Preparation for the Educational Support Services (ESS) Specialist
1. Get to know the child by gathering parent information.
2. Decide who is on the student's "team" and who may need to be added.
3. Start collaborating with the general education teacher.
4. Create a Student Profile to hand out to all teachers working with the student (or the whole staff). The Profile should be short, positive, and honest.
5. Be the team cheerleader.

Preparation for the General Educator
We often hear, "But I never went to school for this!" And that's okay! You're part of a team.
1. Learn as much as possible about the student—both their strengths and the weaknesses. Support will come from the team.
2. Participate in a meeting with parents and the team before the school year begins. Let the parents talk about their child and let the teacher talk about the classroom. This is an important link! Participants should include: parents, general education teacher(s), paraprofessional (as needed), principal, and an ESS teacher who facilitates—but does not dominate—the discussion.
3. Review Student Profile, created by ESS teacher.
4. Complete "Inclusion Support Menu."

Preparation for Paraeducator
1. Get to know the student. Read Student Profile and attend the first planning meeting.
2. Understand the schedule and clearly defined roles and responsibilities, as set by the ESS teacher.
3. Know school policies and procedures.

Preparation and Reminders for ESS Staff Working in an Inclusive Setting
Helping a child work towards independence is a difficult job when you're assigned the task to "help." Remember, independence is the goal.
1. Be the connector: build bridges between the student and the general education teacher. If the paraeducator solves every need, they do a disservice to the student and teacher. Likewise, be the connector between the general education

teacher and parents. Direct parent questions to the general education teacher to encourage interaction.
2. Model good communication skills: if a peer asks you a question say, "I'm not sure, ask [student]..."
3. Use names, avoid terms of endearment (e.g., honey, sweetheart).
4. Let the child take risks. Safety first, but it's okay for them to stumble.
5. Learn to wait. Resist the temptation to do tasks for the student to speed up the process. Know the student's goals and when it's appropriate to take the time for a student to do the task independently.
6. Step back. You are the "secret servant" with the job of facilitating inclusion. This means do whatever is needed in advance to help the child participate to the greatest extent possible.
7. Involve peers. Students are the most under used resource in our schools! They have great ideas.

Preparation for Parents of the Child
1. Share about the child at the meeting: child's history, hopes and dreams, fears, likes and dislikes, strengths and challenges, and what an ideal day at school looks like.
2. Share preferred communication methods with the ESS teacher and general educator(s).
3. Parents, please remember that *you are fully included in the general education scene.* You are a parent helper if your child is in preschool. Your child is expected at general education programs and concerts--just like all the other students. All classroom projects, field trips, and programs will involve your child unless you have made specific arrangements with the teacher.

Preparation for the Peers
Preparing the class is vital to success.
1. Use God's Amazing Puzzle lesson (email Info@allbelong.org) to highlight how each person has strengths and challenges.
2. Share information you gathered from parents (with permission!)—anything that helps the peers better understand and interact with their classmate. Invite questions!
3. Model person-first language.
4. Talk about the student's individual strengths and challenges. Be student-specific, as opposed to labeling characteristics of the diagnosis (i.e. "Kids with autism spectrum disorder usually...").

Preparation for the Child
1. Invite the student to school to explore the environment when the room is empty. Visit the different classrooms the student will spend time in.
2. Introduce a few buddies to the student before school starts. They could join towards the end of the visiting day. Share information about the student and

ACSI Leading Insights

highlight ways they can help the first day (this is a great way to begin peer interactions).
3. Develop a *School Welcome Story* to highlight what will take place the first days of school. Some students benefit from having a short story with pictures.

Preparation for Parents of Peers
Kids will come home from school with stories which can be interpreted best by parents if they are provided with an accurate lens in which to view the situation.
1. Help the parents understand who the student is by sending a letter home. The letter needs to be personal, accurate, and positive. Have the child's parents approve the letter before sending it out.

Preparation for the School Community
Preparing an entire school for the first time can be a fun experience!
1. Use chapels, classroom devotions, or simulation activities to create an understanding of inclusive community. Topics to focus on include: everyone has strengths and challenges; we are more alike than different; and we all have gifts to contribute to God's kingdom.
2. During the year, share stories of how you see God at work in your school as you focus on building inclusive community.
3. Mail out a letter from administration explaining the opportunity and vision of inclusion. Here's an excerpt from a Christian school administrator's letter:

> In the coming weeks, many of our students will see familiar faces and will meet new students. We will be learning more about the fact that each member of the body has different gifts and abilities, but that these parts are essential for a healthy body. **What does that mean for you as parents?** As people with a more mature understanding of the body of Christ, it is important that you partner with us in helping your students understand that every child has different abilities, and every child has difficulties. Some difficulties are more may be more visible than others. We want to focus on celebrating the diverse abilities and not focus on critiquing the difficulties. We need to model to our children the grace that God gives to us. Join me in praying for our school community this year as we continue to provide an excellent, Christ-centered education to all students who walk through our doors, and as we prepare students for service in God's Kingdom, as vital members of the body of Christ.

Sample Inclusion Support Menu

Effective collaboration requires clear communication and defined roles. This menu is one way to provide clear communication as teachers share responsibilities for students. All Belong recommends the educational support services teacher asks the general education teacher to complete this menu at the start of the year.

Teacher's Name _____

Student You Serve _____

Check one or more blanks per section.

Communication: Do you prefer...?

____ A scheduled, weekly time to sit down and meet

____ A scheduled, monthly time to sit down and meet

____ Informal visits to my classroom as needed to address questions and concerns

Learning more: Would you like...?

____ Information on supporting this child

____ Information on your child's specific disability

____ Information on the following topic(s) related to special education:

____ I feel well informed at this point, but will let you know if I need anything

Circle of Friends: (if needed) The number of students in the Circle will depend on what is best for the student. In addition to Circle of Friends meetings, do you prefer...?

____ Hold full class meetings with the help of the special education teacher

____ I will meet with the class on a regular basis and ask support staff to join if needed.

____ Circle of Friends meetings during this part of the school day:

____ I would appreciate or have appreciated the following activities:

Curriculum Adaptations: Would you like...?

____ A folder of work or activities for your room to use as a back-up system for the student

____ Adapted writing or journal folder

____ I want to wait and see

School/Home Notebook: For some students, I have a notebook or Google document that is shared with parents daily. Parents and teachers can write in the notebook or document. Do you prefer...?

____ Support services has reading and writing responsibilities

____ I read the notebook or document, but support staff writes in it

____ I read and write in the notebook or document while support staff does the same

Conferences:

____ I would like to have my own conference with the parents and have the support staff do the same

____ I would like to have a joint 15-minute conference and have support staff meet separately with the parents for 15 minutes

____ I would like to have a joint 30-minute conference

Shaping Our Practice

PERSON-GUIDED TRANSITION PLANNING

CENTER FOR INCLUSIVE EDUCATION

Foundation

Facilitating

Middle School

8th/High School

Tools

ACSI Leading Insights

Foundation: This section provides an overview of the fundamental concepts and values underlying all Person-Guided Planning approaches. A few people at your school need to understand how to facilitate meetings, but the success of the plan often depends on the greater school community understanding and embracing the values and principles surrounding Person-Guided Planning. Without common values, any time spent planning may be misdirected or not accepted, so please do not skip this important step of building a foundation.

A Person-Guided Approach

This begins with the belief that people of all abilities are whole and complete with strengths and gifts that are valued and are needed in the community in which they live and learn. It recognizes each person belongs, and it creates a space where individuals are celebrated for their ability to contribute to the educational community and opportunities to do so are intentionally cultivated. Person-Guided means there is an understanding that learners deserve to be uniquely known and have an active voice in planning for their future. It is with this understanding that specific supports are wrapped around the learner.

Embedded in this approach are All Belong's core beliefs. Directed by the Gospel of Jesus Christ and relying on the Holy Spirit, we believe:

We need diversity of ability to form a complete community

We experience God's love through belonging in community

We bring glory to God when we live, learn, serve, and worship together in interdependent community

Person-Guided Planning

This planning approach is a positive and affirming process that guides the learner and their team to creatively dream and plan for the future. It recognizes the learner has an active role in creating and sharing their vision for the future while expressing what is important now and in the future. Person-Guided Planning builds on the strengths, interests, skills and contributions of the individual to identify action steps that inform day-to-day supports. Research has shown that young people are more likely to be successful as adults if they have experience making their own decisions and choices. It develops an appropriate sense of agency for the learner.

Shaping Our Practice

Approaching transition planning, required by the Individuals with Disabilities Education Act (IDEA), with a person-guided approach ensures that the details of planning focus on what is most important to the learner while recognizing the team of peers, parents, teachers, family or church members, and other invested participants as vital contributors.

Inviting team members into an ever-widening circle of support complements what is beautifully modeled day after day in schools, moving beyond inclusion to creating communities of belonging. These schools are a place where everyone belongs, everyone is cherished and needed, and everyone is recognized as having gifts to share in the body of Christ. With a focus on interdependence, schools realize it is inadequate to develop transition plans that focus solely on the attempt to empower individuals to reach independence. Interdependence means that everyone needs everyone to be the best he or she can be. A Person-Guided transition plan addresses both the growth of individual self-direction and the community in which they live and learn.

The very nature of this approach pushes thinking beyond traditional systems related to standard classes and measurement of academic success. It creates a space where students are celebrated for their ability to contribute to the educational community and opportunities to do so are intentionally cultivated.

System-Centered Approach	Person-Guided Approach
Focuses on the labels/ diagnosis/ deficits	Focused on strengths, skills, abilities
Focuses on independence	Focus on interdependence
Communicates **about** the learner	Communicating **with** the learner
Plans **for** the learner	Planning **with** the learner
Focuses on what the learner can't do	Focus on what the learner can do
Fits the learner into a program or system	Cultivate new opportunities
Focuses on medical or clinical diagnosis	Personal profile of strengths, likes, dislikes
Places an overemphasis on clinical strategies or fitting into program goals	Emphasis on dreams, desires, and meaningful experiences
Decides things are done "that way" because it works	Things are done "that way" because it works for the learner
Views family members and community are peripheral	Family and community members are true partners

all belong — Foundation — Page 2

ACSI Leading Insights

Person-Guided Plan for Belonging

Grounded in the concept of I Corinthians that all individuals are needed for a community to be complete, All Belong understands inclusion as creating communities of belonging. Rather than having a presence in a community, persons with a disability label should be a vibrant part of community and developing the reciprocal nature of giving and receiving in relationship with others.

Person-Guided Plan for Belonging

Five Essential Experiences for People

1. Belonging in ordinary places

The learner has the right to take part in community life and to live and spend leisure time with others.
- How can we increase the presence of a learner in the life of the school community and beyond?
- Does the student live, work, learn, and play confidently in ordinary school-related settings?

2. Belonging within relationship

The learner has the right to experience valued relationships.
- How can we expand and deepen people's friendships?
- Does the student have real and meaningful relationships and know who they can depend on?

3. Belonging through dignity of valued roles

The learner has the right to be valued and not treated as a second-class citizen.
- How can we enhance the reputation people have and increase the number of valued ways people can contribute?
- Do others view the student as a whole person (e.g., history, capacities, dreams) whose gifts are needed and valued?

4. Belonging through agency

The learner has the right to make choices, both large and small, in one's life.
- How can we help people have more control and choice in life?
- Does the learner have the freedom, supports, information, and assistance to make the same choices as their peers and are they learning to make wiser choices over time?

5. Belonging through contributing

The learner has the right to learn new skills and participate in meaningful activities with whatever assistance is required.
- How can we assist people to develop more competencies and contribute their unique gifts?
- Do others see the student as one who is cherished and needed and recognize the gifts they have to share in the body of Christ?

all belong — Foundation

Shaping Our Practice

Circle of Support

It is essential to include individuals who are familiar with the abilities, interests, and needs of the learner in the Person-Guided Planning Process. These "natural supports" can be family members, friends, former teachers, neighbors, or other individuals who know the leaner well and want to come alongside the learner in a way that makes a difference in both of their lives. Building the circle of support with both professionals and natural supports will provide access to a broad range of opportunities at school and in the community.

Think about the circle as a life support system. We all have them. These are the people we depend on to help us make decisions, navigate tough times, and enjoy spending time with. All people are created for relationships. Circles are for everyone. With this in mind, we intentionally build this support system around the learner. This is the core to everything else.

Identifying Circle of Support team:
- Ask the learner! Who is important to you? Who can you count on?
- Create accountability! There needs to be a commitment from a core team who meets regularly.
- Include others! Other people may join over time based on circumstances (e.g., share a class with the learner, involved in after-school activities, new friendship)

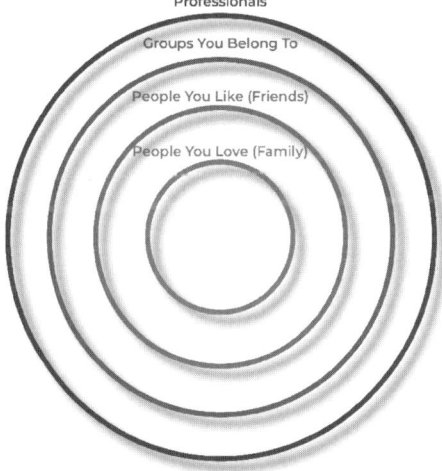

all belong — Foundation — Page 4

ACSI Leading Insights

Facilitating: Facilitating the Person-Guided Planning Process is a unique opportunity for faith-based schools to truly celebrate the uniqueness of the individual as an image bearer of God. This isn't simply doing special education in a Christian school. The approach in which you truly embrace the uniqueness of this learner, and the hope-filled manner that you attend to these delicate subjects, will minister in a profound way to the family. Remember, bringing their newborn home from the hospital seems like just yesterday to these caregivers; this is a tender process that often involves some grieving before arriving at hope-filled solutions. It is a good time to imagine walking in their shoes. From scheduling to the post meeting, let professionalism and sensitivity guide the specific plan development and communication with all involved in the life of the student from general education teachers to peers.

The Facilitator Role

Effective Coordination
- Comprehends the Person-Guided Planning Process and invests in the outcomes of the plan
- Approaches tasks in a creative and flexible manner
- Provides the structure and process at each meeting and encourages participation by all members
- Ensures plan remains current as goals and preferences evolve
- Monitors and tracks progress
- Organizes time and resources

Person Directed
- Accommodates the person's style of interaction and preferences in the planning process
- Focuses on what is important to the person
- Helps shape the dream of the person by recognizing possibilities, naming the desires within the person and imagining concrete ways to close the gap between dream and reality.
- Attending, responding, and understanding how best to build upon a person's strengths and gifts

Effective Communication
- Engages in deep and active listening skills
- Poses questions to encourage creative problem solving and collaboration
- Values everyone's contributions
- Helps the group celebrate success and accomplishments, and grieves over setbacks

Fosters Connections
- Supports the learner and works to establish, grow, and maintain a support network
- Cultivates a climate of respect, acceptance, trust, and cohesion among participants
- Connects to formal and informal (natural) support

all belong | Facilitating

Shaping Our Practice

Timely Discussion Topics: Middle School Transition Planning

Middle School Transition Planning: Student

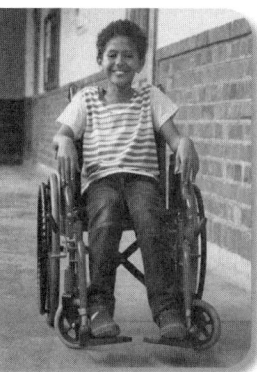

- What progress in the learner's basic academic skills and study habits can be noted?
- What are the most valuable academic supports the learner is receiving, and will they be continued in the high school setting?
- How might the learner's strengths/challenges look in the high school setting?
- How does the learner need to grow to succeed in the high school (e.g., independence and how they navigate the day)?
- Do the parents understand the difference between accommodations and modifications?
- Do the parents understand the difference between a certificate of completion and a high school diploma? Do they understand the difference in impact upon services between earning one versus the other?
- Do the parents understand a personalized curriculum?
- What middle school and/or high school standardized testing will the student participate in?

Middle School Transition Planning: Belonging

- How can we assure the feeling of belonging at the next level?
- What contribution is the learner making as an image bearer to this community (e.g., service, love, and mission)?
- What middle school opportunities can the learner continue into high school?
- **Invited:** Think about inviting the learner to participate in new opportunities.
- **Welcomed:** How does the learner feel welcomed?
- **Needed:** Where can the learner serve and feel needed?
- **Known:** Do peers know *about* the learner, or do they truly know them?

Timely Discussion Topics: High School Transition Planning

9th - 10th Grade Planning: Student

- Does the learner have a clear picture of his/her strengths and challenges and understand God's unique gift in him/her?
- How might the learner's strengths/challenges look in the (next grade) setting?
- What contribution is the learner making as an image bearer to this community (e.g., service, love, and mission)?
  - How will the learner continue contributing when he/she leaves high school?
- Does the learner have more than one identified plan for post-high?

9th - 10th Grade Planning: Community

- Are the parents aware of resources available in your community (e.g., advocacy agencies and county human services agencies)?
  - Are they desirous of a pre-employment appointment?
  - What level of independence do the parents picture for their young adult ten years from now?
  - What are the related financial considerations?
  - Is the young adult embraced by a network of support in addition to the immediate family?
  - Have the parents carefully considered the issue of learner driving and transportation needs?
- Has the student visited at least two possible program options?
  - What entry requirements exist at present?
- Does the level of student services align with their post-high transition plan?

9th - 10th Grade Planning: Belonging

- What volunteer/work experiences engage the student?
- What changes can we anticipate and plan for?
- As the learner considers future plans, how are skills and support needs progressing?
- Has the learner compared the accommodations/modifications probable at the post-high level with those daily depended upon in high school?
- How will student support structures change after high school?
  - How can we best prepare for this?

Shaping Our Practice

Timely Discussion Topics: High School Transition Planning

11th-12th Grade Planning: Student

- What goals does the learner still need to accomplish to be prepared for his/her top choice?
- Have the parents considered and researched the differences between a legal power of attorney and guardianship?
  - Have they considered application for Social Security Income?
  - Do they know the difference between an ABLE account and a Special Needs Trust Fund?

11th-12th Grade Planning: Community

- Have parents explored the resources of Community Mental Health and other community resources?
- Has the learner revisited top post-high options?
  - Can the student meet the requirements?
  - Which one is the best fit?
  - How will he/she meet these goals?
  - What supports are needed?

11th-12th Grade Planning: Belonging

- Are others who know the learner best supportive of his/her post high choices? Will this be an appropriate challenge?

Hebrews 10:24–25 "And let us consider how we may spur one another on toward love and good deeds, not giving up meeting together, as some are in the habit of doing, but encouraging one another—and all the more as you see the Day approaching."

For Further Reading

Anderson, David W. 2013. *Reaching Out and Bringing In: Ministry To and With Persons with Disabilities*. Bloomington, IN: WestBow Press.

Baglieri, Susan and Arthur Shapiro. 2012. *Disability Studies and the Inclusive Classroom: Critical Practices for Creating Least Restrictive Attitudes*. New York, NY: Routledge.

Barringer, Mary-Dean, Craig Pohlman and Michele Robinson. 2010. *Schools for All Kinds of Minds: Boosting Student Success by Embracing Learning Variation*. San Francisco: Jossey-Bass.

Bolt, Sarah. 2009. *Your Feet, My Shoes: Activities to Help Children in Grades 1-8 Understand and Include Peers with Disabilities*. Wyoming, MI: CLC Network.

Carter, Erik W. 2010. *Including People with Disabilities in Faith Communities: A Guide for Service Providers, Families and Congregations*. Baltimore, MD: Paul H. Brookes Publishing.

Danforth, Scott. 2014. *Becoming a Great Inclusive Educator*. New York: Peter Lang.

Forbes, Heather T. 2013. *Help for Billy: A Beyond Consequences Approach to Helping Children in the Classroom*. Cork: BookBaby.

Greene, Ross W. 2014. *Lost at School: Why Our Kids with Behavioral Challenges are Falling Through the Cracks and How We Can Help Them*. New York: Scribner.

---. 2005. *The Explosive Child*. New York: Quill.

Hattie, John. 2013. *Visible Learning and the Science of How We Learn*. New York: Routledge.

Hubach, Stephanie O. 2020. *Same Lake, Different Boat: Coming Alongside People Touched by Disability*. Phillipsburg, NJ: P&R Publishing.

Kranowitz, Carol Stock. 2011. *The Out-of-Sync Child: Recognizing and Coping with Sensory Processing Disorder*. New York, NY: Paw Prints.

Lane, Julie M. and Quentin P. Kinnison. 2014. *Welcoming Children with Special Needs: Empowering Christian Special Education through Purpose, Policies, and Procedures*. Bloomington, IN: WestBow.

The Barbara J. Newman Canon:
- *Inclusion Awareness Kit*. Wyoming, MI: CLC Network.
- 2107. *Nuts & Bolts of Inclusive Education*. Wyoming, MI: CLC Network.
- 2012. *Helping Kids Include Kids with Disabilities*. Grand Rapids, MI: Faith Alive Christian Resources.
- 2015. *Accessible Gospel, Inclusive Worship*. Wyoming, MI: CLC Network.
- 2009. *Body Building*, 2nd ed. Wyoming, MI: CLC Network.

- 2009. *Circle of Friends Manual*. Wyoming, MI: CLC Network.
- 2006. *Autism and Your Church*. Grand Rapids, MI: Friendship Ministries.

Rose, Todd. 2017. *The End of Average: How We Succeed in a World that Values Sameness*. New York: HarperOne.

Winstrom, David. 2017. *I Choose Adam: Nothing "Special" Please*. United States: Lightning Tree Creative Media.

References

Introduction

ACSI. 2019. *2018-2019 Tuition and Salary Survey: Member Report*. Colorado Springs, CO: Author.

Part I: Philosophy and Research

2. Creating Communities of Belonging

Barkley, Katey. 2017. "Creating a Culture of Inclusion at Allendale Christian School." Wyoming, MI: All Belong. Available at: https://allbelong.org/allendale-christian-school/.

Barkley, Katey. 2019. "Belonging Among Friends: A Graduation Reflection." Wyoming, MI: All Belong. Accessed March 25, 2021. https://allbelong.org/belonging-among-friends/.

Carter, Erik William. 2018. "Supporting the Social Lives of Secondary Students with Severe Disabilities: Critical Elements for Effective Intervention." *Journal of Emotional and Behavioral Disorders* 26(1): 52-61.

Carter, Erik William, Elizabeth E. Biggs, and Thomas L. Boehm. 2016. "Being Present Versus Having a Presence: Dimensions of Belonging for Young People with Disabilities and Their Families." *Christian Education Journal* 13(1): 127-146.

Danforth, Scot. 2014. *Becoming a Great Inclusive Educator*. New York: Peter Lang Publishing

Dombrowski, Elizabeth L. 2017. *Welcomed into Community*. Wyoming, MI: All Belong. Retrieved from https://allbelong.org/welcomed-into-community/.

Hunt, David, and Deani Van Pelt. 2019. *Who Chooses Independent Schools in British Columbia and Why?*

Hamilton, ON: Cardus. Available at: https://www.cardus.ca/research/education/reports/who-chooses-independent-schools-in-british-columbia-and-why/.

Hussar, Bill., Jijun Zhang, Sarah Hein, Ke Wang, Ashley Roberts, Jiashan Cui, Mary Smith, Farrah B. Mann, Amy Barmer, and Rita Dilag, 2020. *The Condition of Education*. Washington, DC: U.S. Department of Education. Available at: https://nces.ed.gov/pubsearch/pubsinfo.asp?pubid=2020144.

Timpe, Kevin. 2018. *Disability and Inclusive Communities*. Grand Rapids: Calvin University.

Ziegler, Maureen, Amy Matthews, Margie Mayberry, Jamie Owen-DeSchryver, and Erik William Carter. 2020. "From Barriers to Belonging: Promoting Inclusion and Relationships Through Peer to Peer Programs." *Teaching Exceptional Children* 52(6): 426-434.

3. A Review of the Research on Inclusive Christian Education

Anderson, David. 2003. "Special Education as Reconciliation." *Journal of Education and Christian Belief* 7(1): 23–36.

Anderson, David. 2006a. "Special Education as Spiritual Warfare." *International Christian Community of Teacher Educators Journal* 2(1): 1-7.

Anderson, David. 2006b. "Inclusion and Interdependence: Students with Special Needs in the Regular Classroom." *Journal of Education and Christian Belief* 10(1): 43–59.

Anderson, David. 2010. "Biblical Justice and Inclusive Education." *Journal of Religion, Disability & Health* 14(4): 338–354.

Anderson, David. 2011. "Hospitable Classrooms: Biblical Hospitality and Inclusive Education." *Journal of Education and Christian Belief* 15(1): 13-27.

Bayer, Wendy W. 2017. "A Transcendental Phenomenological Study Examining Parents' Perceptions Regarding the Enrollment of a Child with Learning Differences in an NILD Program in a K-12 Christian School." EdD diss., Liberty University.

Broughman, Stephen P. and Kathleen W. Pugh. 2019. *Characteristics of Private Schools in the United States: Results From the 2017-18 Private School Universe Survey*, distributed by US Department of Education, National Center for Education Statistics.

Burke, Meghan M. and Megan M. Griffin. 2016. "Students with Developmental Disabilities in Catholic Schools: Examples in Primary and Secondary Settings." *Journal of Catholic Education* 19(3): 197–220.

Cappiello, Leslie W. 2013. "Teaching Methods and Strategies Used in a Christian High School for Students with Emotional and Behavioral Disorders." PhD diss., Capella University. ProQuest LLC.

Carlson, Mary. 2014. "Aquinas on Inclusion: Using the Good Doctor and Catholic Social Teaching to Build a Moral Case for Inclusion in Catholic Schools for Children with Special Needs." *Journal of Catholic Education* 18(1): 62–78.

Contreras, Jennifer C. 2013. "Including Exceptional Children in a Christian Learning Community: New Narratives in Special Education." EdD diss., University of San Francisco.

Cookson, Gary and Samuel Smith. 2011. "Establishing Special Education Programs: Experiences of Christian School Principals." *Journal of Research on Christian Education* 20(3): 239–253.

Craig, Kristi-Lynn. 2010. "A Historical Analysis of Special Education Services in Conservative Christian Schools

Since 1950." Master's thesis, Cedarville University.

DeFiore, Leonard. 2006. "The State of Special Education in Catholic Schools." *Journal of Catholic Education* 9(4).

Eigenbrood, Rick. 2005. "A Survey Comparing Special Education Services for Students with Disabilities in Rural Faith-Based and Public School Settings." *Remedial and Special Education* 26(1): 16–24.

Eigenbrood, Rick. 2010. "IDEA Requirements for Children with Disabilities in Faith-Based Schools: Implications for Practice." *Journal of Religion, Disability & Health* 14(4): 393–409.

Hoeksema, Thomas. 2007. "Radical Shifts: New Ways of Thinking About Disability and Schooling." *Christian Educators Journal* 46(3).

Lai, Yue Sum Sharon and Kaili Chen Zhang. 2014. "A Comparison on Inclusive Practices for Children with Special Needs in Faith-Based Kindergartens in Hong Kong." *Journal of Religion and Health* 53(3): 809–824.

Lane, Julie M. 2011. "Special Education in Christian Schools: Post-Professional Development Support." EdD diss., Pepperdine University.

Lane, Julie M. 2017. "Special Education Staffing and Service Models in Christian Schools." *Journal of Research on Christian Education* 26(3): 225–236.

Lane, Julie M. and David R. Jones. 2014. "Special Education Professional Development in Christian Schools." *Journal of the Christian Institute on Disability* 3(2): 45–68.

---2015a. "Children with Special Needs: Enrollment Practices in Christian Schools." *Journal of the Christian Institute on*

Disability 4(2): 99–112.

Lane, Julie M. and David R. Jones. 2015b. "Child Find Practices in Christian Schools." *Journal of Research on Christian Education* 24(3): 212–223.

Lane, Julie M., Quentin P. Kinnison, and Ancantha Ellard. 2019. "Creating Inclusive and Hospitable Christian Schools: Three Case Studies." *Journal of Disability & Religion* 23(1): 37–58.

Long, Thomas J., and Merylann Schuttloffel. 2006. "A Rationale for Special Education in Catholic Schools." *Journal of Catholic Education* 9(4).

Mercer, David. 2015. "Educating Students with Disabilities in Regional Independent Christian Schools of Queensland: An Analysis of School Policies." *Journal of the Christian Institute on Disability* 4(2): 13–37.

Mitchell, David. 2015. "Inclusive Education is a Multi-Faceted Concept." *Center for Educational Policy Studies Journal* 5(1): 9–30.

National Institute for Learning Development. 2020. NILD home page. https://www.nild.org/.

Ningham, Matthew, Karen Hutching, Diane Fogarty, and Victoria Graf. 2017. "Providing Access for Students with Moderate Disabilities: An Evaluation of a Professional Development Program at a Catholic Elementary School." *Journal of Catholic Education* 21(1): 138–170.

Oosterhuis, Alyce. 2002. "The Development of a Christian Ideology of Inclusive Education." *Journal of Research on Christian Education* 11(1): 5–31.

Osborne, Allan G., Philip Dimattia, and Charles J. Russo. 1998. "Legal Considerations in Providing Special Education

Services in Parochial Schools." *Exceptional Children* 64(3): 385-395.

Paxton-Buursma, Debra. 2007. "Inclusive Classrooms: A Matter of Head and Heart." *Christian Educators Journal* 46(3).

Pirner, Manfred L. 2015. "Inclusive Education—a Christian Perspective to an 'Overlapping Consensus.'" *International Journal of Christianity & Education* 19(3): 229–239.

Poon-McBrayer, Kim Fong, and Ping-man Wong. 2013. "Inclusive Education Services for Children and Youth with Disabilities: Values, Roles and Challenges of School Leaders." *Children and Youth Services Review* 35(9): 1520–1525.

Pudlas, Kenneth A. 2004. "Inclusive Education: Will They Know We Are Christians." *Journal of Research on Christian Education* 13(1): 61–79.

Russo, Charles J., Gerald M. Cattaro, and Allan G. Osborne. 1999. "State Aid to Religiously Affiliated, Non-public Schools: An Emerging Trend or Same Old Same Old?" *Journal of Research on Christian Education* 8(2): 267–289.

Russo, Charles J., Allan G. Osborne, Joseph D. Massucci, and Gerald M. Cattaro. 2011. "The Legal Rights of Students with Disabilities in Christian Schools." *Journal of Research on Christian Education* 20(3): 254–280.

Sargeant, Marcel and Donna Berkner. 2015. "Seventh-Day Adventist Teachers' Perceptions of Inclusion Classrooms and Identification of Challenges to Their Implementation." *Journal of Research on Christian Education* 24(3): 224–251.

Scanlan, Martin. 2009a. "Moral, Legal, and Functional Dimensions of Inclusive Service Delivery in Catholic Schools." *Catholic Education: A Journal of Inquiry and Practice* 12(4): 536–552.

Scanlan, Martin. 2009b. "Leadership Dynamics Promoting Systemic Reform for Inclusive Service Delivery." *Journal of School Leadership* 19(6): 622–660.

Stegink, Philip. (2010). "Disability to Community: A Journey to Create Inclusive Christian Schools." *Journal of Religion, Disability & Health*, 14(4): 368–381.

Stymeist, Melissa, and Fred Ramirez. 2019. "Bible Theory or Biblical Living: What are Christian Schools Providing for Families With Children With Special Needs?" *International Christian Community of Teacher Educators Journal* 14(2): 17.

Taylor, Shanon S. 2005. "Special Education and Private Schools: Principals' Points of View." *Remedial and Special Education* 26(5): 281–296.

United States Department of Education. 2019. *Fast Facts: Students With Disabilities*. Washington, DC: National Center for Education Statistics.

Van Dyk, William. 2010. "Changing School Culture at Zeeland Christian School." *Journal of Religion, Disability & Health* 14(4): 382–384.

Part II: Perspectives on Inclusive Education

5. The Parent Perspective

Craven, Michael. 2010. "The Christian Conquest of Pagan Rome." *Crosswalk* (blog), November 8, 2010. Available at: https://www.crosswalk.com/blogs/michael-craven/the-christian-conquest-of-pagan-rome-11640691.html.

Hoekema, Anthony A. 1986. *Created in God's Image*. Grand Rapids, MI: William B. Eerdmans Publishing Company.

The Westminster Assembly. 1992. *The Westminster Confession of Faith: With Proof Texts*. Horsham, PA: Great Commission Publications.

Part III: Shaping Our Practice

7. The Inclusion Journey: From Program to Identity

All Belong. 2018. *Brand Guide*. Retrieved from https://allbelong.org/media/All-Belong-Brand-Guide.pdf. Wyoming, MI: Author.

---. 2020. *Person-Guided Transition Planning Toolkit*. [electronic resource]. Wyoming, MI: Author.

Aspy, Ruth and Barry G. Grossman. 2008. *The Ziggurat Model: A Framework for Designing Comprehensive Interventions for Individuals with High-Functioning Autism and Asperger's Syndrome*. Shawnee Mission, KS: Autism Asperger Publishing Company.

Barringer, Mary-Dean, Craig Pohlman, and Michele Robinson. 2010. *Schools for All Kinds of Minds: Boosting Student Success by Embracing Learning Variation*. San Francisco, CA: John Wiley & Sons.

Dombrowski, Elizabeth. 2017. "Donor Profile: Schreur Family." Inclusive. Wyoming, MI: All Belong. Retrieved from https://allbelong.org/schreur-family/.

Greene, Ross W. 2018. "Transforming School Discipline: Shifting from Power and Control to Collaboration and Problem Solving." *Childhood Education* 94(4): 22-27.

Lane, Julie M. 2017. "Special Education Staffing and Service Models in Christian Schools." *Journal of Research on Christian Education* 26(3): 225–236.

Paxton-Buursma, Debra. 2007. "Inclusive Classrooms: A Matter of Head and Heart." *Christian Educators Journal* 46(3): 10-15.

Riester-Wood, Toni. 2015. "Peers Supporting an Inclusive School Climate." *Inclusive School Network*. Retrieved from http://inclusiveschools.org/peers-supporting-an-inclusive-school-climate/.

8: Reimagining Finance and Sustainability: From Limits to Possibilities

All Belong. 2018. "Including Isaac." YouTube, April 3, 2018. Available at: https://www.youtube.com/watch?v=bJV19gXl9zA.

Barkley, Katie. 2019. *All Belong Brand Guide*. Wyoming, MI: All Belong. Available at: https://allbelong.org/about-us/brand/all-belong-brand-guide/.

Claypool, Mark and John McLaughlin. 2017. *Why Improving America's Understanding of Special Needs Will Lead to More Educational Choice*. Indianapolis, IN: EdChoice. Available at: https://www.edchoice.org/engage/improving-americas-understanding-special-needs-will-lead-educational-choice/.

Danforth, Scot, ed. 2014. *Becoming a Great Inclusive Educator*. New York: Peter Lang Publishing, Inc.

DiPerna, Paul, Andrew D. Catt, and Michael Shaw. 2020. *K-12 Education and School Choice Reforms: 2020 Schooling in America*. Indianapolis, IN: EdChoice. Available at: https://www.edchoice.org/wp-content/uploads/2020/08/K%E2%80%9312-Education-and-School-Choice-Reforms-FINAL.pdf.

Greene, Jay P. 2007. "Fixing Special Education." *Peabody Journal of Education* 82(4): 703-723.

Greene, Jay P. and Greg Forster. 2003. *Vouchers for Special Education*

Students: An Evaluation of Florida's McKay Scholarship Program. Civic Report 38. New York: Center for Civic Innovation at the Manhattan Institute. Available at: https://media4.manhattan-institute.org/pdf/cr_32.pdf.

Greene, Jay P. and Marcus A. Winters. 2007. "Debunking a Special Education Myth." *Education Next* 7(2). Available at: https://www.educationnext.org/debunking-a-special-education-myth/.

Greene, Jay P. and Stuart Buck. 2010. "The Case for Special Education Vouchers." *Education Next* 10(2). Available at: https://www.educationnext.org/the-case-for-special-education-vouchers/.

Hoeksema, Thomas B. 2007. "Radical Shifts: New Ways of Thinking about Disability and Schooling." *Christian Educators' Journal* 46(3).

Hussar, Bill, Jijun Zhang, Sarah Hein, Ke Wang, Ashley Roberts, Jiashan Cui, and Mary Smith, 2020. *The Condition of Education* (NCES 2020-144). Washington, DC: National Center for Education Statistics. Available at: https://nces.ed.gov/pubs2020/2020144.pdf.

Laird, Lorelei. 2017. "Supreme Court rules schools must provide special ed students a chance to make 'meaningful progress.'" *ABA Journal*, March 22, 2017.

Nouwen, Henri J. M. 2010. *A Spirituality of Fundraising.* The Henri J. M. Nouwen Spirituality Series, edited by John S. Mogabgab. Nashville, TN: Upper Room Books.

Sirleaf, Ellen Johnson. 2011. "Harvard University Commencement Address." *Harvard Magazine*. Available at: https://harvardmagazine.com/2011/05/ellen-johnson-sirleaf-commencement-speech.

Swaner, Lynn E. and Matthew H. Lee. 2020. *Christian Schools and COVID-19: 2020-2021 School Year Profile*. Colorado Springs, CO: Association of Christian Schools International.

Swaner, Lynn E., Charlotte A. Marshall, and Sheri A. Tesar. 2019. *Flourishing Schools: Research on Christian School Culture and Community*. Colorado Springs, CO: Association of Christian Schools International.

U.S. Department of Education. 2019. "Students with disabilities, inclusion of." Fast Facts. Washington, DC: National Center for Education Statistics. Available at: https://nces.ed.gov/fastfacts/display.asp?id=59.

Van Dyk, William. 2010. "Changing School Culture at Zeeland Christian School." *Journal of Religion, Disability & Health* 14(4): 382-384.

Varga, Shannon, Albert Cheng, Emily Coady, Yawei Huang, Shea Martin, Cathleen Donohue, and Anna Skubel, 2021. *Choices and Challenges: Florida Parents' Experiences with the State's McKay and Gardiner Scholarship Programs for Students with Disabilities*. Boston, MA: CERES Institute for Children & Youth. Available at: https://ceresinstitute.org/wp-content/uploads/2021/04/ChoicesChallengesREPORT.pdf.

Weidner, Virginia R. and Carolyn D. Herrington. 2006. "Are Parents Informed Consumers: Evidence from the Florida McKay Scholarship Program." *Peabody Journal of Education* 81(1): 27-56.

About the Authors

Dr. Thomas Boehm's work is situated at the intersection of disability and faith. In the summer of 2019, he helped launch and leads a new Center for Faith and Disability at Wheaton College. Since 2015, he has served as Wheaton's Ann Haskins Associate Professor of Special Education and the Coordinator of the Special Education Program. In 2009, Dr. Boehm founded and continues to direct Faith for ALL, a nonprofit dedicated to promoting and supporting inclusive faith communities. Dr. Boehm's research and writing focus on building inclusive community within schools and congregations to improve family quality of life for both people with and without disability.

Dr. Erik Carter is the Cornelius Vanderbilt Professor of Special Education at Vanderbilt University. His research and teaching focuses on evidence-based strategies for supporting inclusion and valued roles in school, work, community, and congregational settings for students with intellectual and developmental disabilities. He is especially passionate about equipping churches and schools to be communities of belonging for those with disabilities.

Elizabeth Lucas Dombrowski is the executive director of All Belong, equipping congregations and schools to glorify God through purposeful, innovative inclusion of persons of varied abilities. All Belong partners with Christ-centered schools across the country to support their students, and welcomes conversations and questions about inclusion of students of all abilities. She holds an MBA from Grand Valley State University.

Dr. Matthew H. Lee is ACSI's Director of Research. Dr. Lee is co-editor of the book *Religious Liberty and Education* and has published numerous research articles related to school choice outcomes, private school leadership, and educational program evaluation. Dr. Lee's work at ACSI involves building on ACSI's groundbreaking Flourishing Schools Research and sustainability initiatives, as well as developing new initiatives that will undergird ACSI's thought leadership in Christian education.

Dr. Kate Strater is an assistant professor of special education at Calvin University. After 18 years in public education serving in a variety of teaching, consulting, and administrative roles, she now serves as a teacher educator in the field of special education. Her areas of research include developing individualized supports for self-determination, quality of life, and goal attainment for individuals with intellectual and developmental disability. She is passionate about transition planning and growing inclusive employment and post-secondary education opportunities.

About the Series Editor

Dr. Lynn E. Swaner is the chief strategy and innovation officer at ACSI, where she leads initiatives and develops strategies to address compelling questions and challenges facing Christian education. Dr. Swaner serves as a Cardus Senior Fellow and is the co-author or editor of multiple books on Christian education, including *Flourishing Together: A Christian Vision for Students, Educators, and Schools* (forthcoming 2021 from Wm. B. Eerdmans Publishing) and *MindShift: Catalyzing Change in Christian Education*. Prior to joining ACSI, she served as a professor of education and a Christian school administrator in New York.

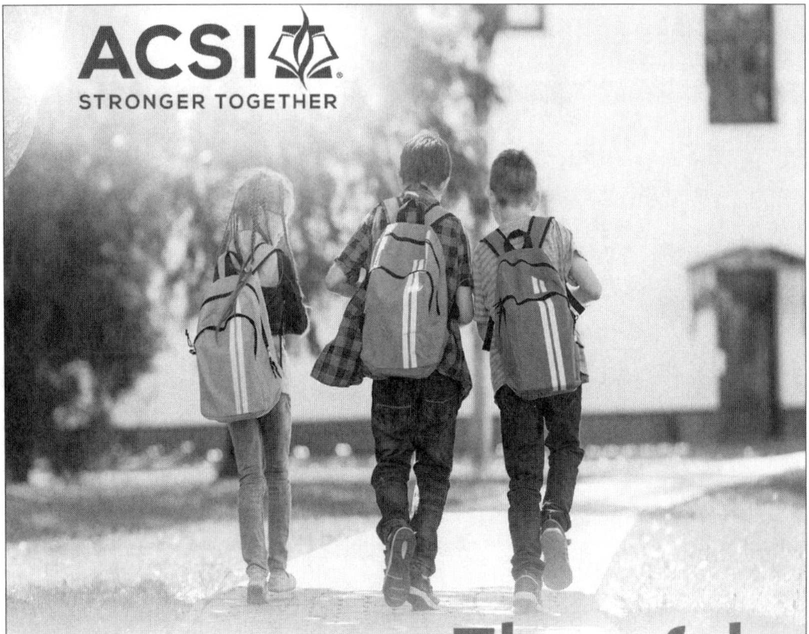

It's Time to Flourish

Think for a moment: in 100 years, what legacy do you want to leave for the students who sat in your classrooms? ACSI wants to come alongside you and help your school community flourish how God intends—biblically.

ACSI has been leading Christ-centered education toward excellence for more than 40 years, always seeking to understand what truly impacts and improves a Christian school. Through a multi-year endeavor, ACSI Research identified 35 constructs that support five primary domains of flourishing, which contribute to a school community marked by healthy spiritual, emotional, and cultural characteristics. This research was validated by a rigorous independent review and has blossomed into the ACSI Flourishing Initiative, which aligns ACSI Research, Professional Development, and Accreditation with a focus on flourishing students, educators, and Christian schools.

ACSI *Leading Insights: Special Education* advances Christ-centered education by focusing on schools' responsiveness to special needs, which is a validated construct in the flourishing domain of Expertise & Resources.

To learn more, please visit acsi.org/flourishing.